the
KNOW IT ALL
Resource Book for Kids*

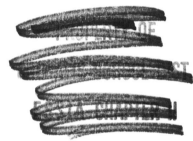

Patricia R. Peterson

* and grown-ups, too!

Dear Boys and Girls,

Need help, but the teacher's busy?
Try THE KNOW IT ALL.

THE KNOW IT ALL contains definitions and "how to do it" examples about most subjects and topics you study at school.

Easy to use:
- Every entry is listed alphabetically.
- Every entry includes its meaning and, often, examples and an illustration.
- Use THE KNOW IT ALL like a dictionary.

That's all there is to it!

THE KNOW IT ALL will become one of your best friends.

Have fun learning!

Mrs. Peterson

the
KNOW IT ALL
Resource Book for Kids*

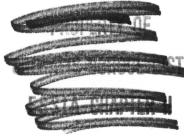

Patricia R. Peterson

* and grown-ups, too!

The KNOW IT ALL Resource Book for Kids*
*and grown-ups, too!

© 1989 Zephyr Press

ISBN 0-9137057-45-4

23308

Book Design and Production: Kathleen Koopman
Editor: Kathryn Ring

Zephyr Press
P.O. Box 13448
Tucson, AZ 85732-3448

※

To

Grandma + Grandpa

Thank you!

Dear Boys and Girls,

Need help, but the teacher's busy?
Try THE KNOW IT ALL.

THE KNOW IT ALL contains definitions
and "how to do it" examples about most
subjects and topics you study at school.

Easy to use:
- Every entry is listed alphabetically.
- Every entry includes its meaning
  and, often, examples and an illustration.
- Use THE KNOW IT ALL like a dictionary.

That's all there is to it!

THE KNOW IT ALL will become one
of your best friends.

Have fun learning!

Mrs. Peterson

CONTENTS

H

I

K

L

M

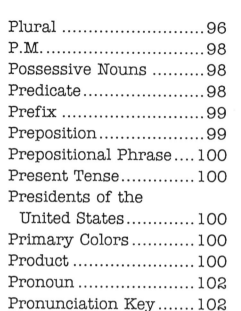

A

a-an-and

The words *a* and *an* are used as adjectives before other adjectives, adverbs, and singular nouns. A singular noun means one—one person, one place, or one thing.

The word *and* is used to connect words, phrases, or clauses.

 **RULES**

- Use *a* before words beginning with a consonant.

    Examples: a funny clown
    a banana

- Use *an* before words beginning with vowels.

    Examples: an elephant
    an old lady

- Use *and* to connect nouns, verbs, adjectives, adverbs, phrases, or clauses.

    Examples: salt *and* pepper
    in the house *and* in the yard
    Paul played, *and* Jim studied.

abbreviation

A shortened form of a word or phrase. Abbreviations are usually followed by periods. Some abbreviations must be capitalized.

* Abbreviations for names of states in the U.S.A. are not followed by a period.

COMMON ABBREVIATIONS

A.D.	anno Domini
adj.	adjective
adv.	adverb
a.m.	ante meridiem; before noon
anon.	anonymous
ant.	antonym
Ave.	Avenue
B.C.	before Christ
biog.	biography
Blvd.	Boulevard
Capt.	Captain
cm	centimeter
C.O.D.	collect on delivery
conj.	conjunction
cont.	continued
D.C.	District of Columbia
dept.	department
Dr.	Doctor
doz.	dozen
etc.	et cetera; and so forth
fig.	figure
ft.	foot
gal.	gallon
Gov.	Governor
ht.	height
illus.	illustration
in.	inch
Jr.	Junior
k	kilo
kg	kilogram
l	liter
lb.	pound
liq.	liquid
mi.	mile
m.p.h.	miles per hour
Mr.	Mister
Mrs.	Mistress
Ms.	Miss or Mrs.
n.	noun
oz.	ounce
p.m.	post meridiem; after noon
P.O.	post office
P.S.	postscript
pt.	pint
qt.	quart
Rd.	Road
Rev.	Reverend
St.	Street
syn.	synonym
U.S.A.	United States of America
v.	verb
V.I.P.	Very Important Person
vol.	volume
yd.	yard

Also see **United States of America.**

accent mark
[′]

A mark used in a pronunciation guide to show which syllable of a word is said or heard loudest. That syllable is called the primary accented syllable.

> **Examples:** pen′ cil
> a - bove′
> re - mem′ ber

✳ **Underlining accented syllables will help you pronounce the word more easily.**

acute angle

See angle.

A.D.

An abbreviation for the Latin words anno Domini (in the year of the Lord), meaning the time in years *after* the birth of Christ.

A.D. 1989 means one thousand nine hundred eighty-nine years *after* the birth of Christ.

✳ **A.D. is often omitted. A date written without the letters is assumed to be A.D.**

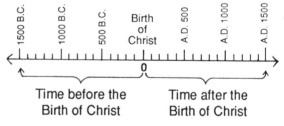

Also see **B.C.**

addend

A number to be added. Any of a set of numbers to be added.

> **Examples:**
>
> 7
> +2
>
> The numbers 7 and 2 are addends.

$$
\begin{array}{r}
3 \\
9 \\
+12 \\
\end{array}
$$

The numbers 3, 9, and 12 are addends.

addition

The process of adding a number to one or more numbers. The answer is called the sum.

Example:

$$
\begin{array}{r}
5 \\
2 \\
+3 \\
\hline
10 \\
\end{array}
$$

or 5 + 2 + 3 = 10

The number 10 is the sum.

✳ **Other words used in addition**

plus	increase or add
sum	how many altogether
total	the sum; how much was added

Also see **casting out nines.**

addressing an envelope

See **letter writing (business).**

adjective

A word that describes or tells about a person, place, or thing. Adjectives tell what kind, which one, or how many.

Examples:

What Kind	Which One	How Many
tiny toes	*that* box	*several* men
large city	*this* house	*few* pigs
bright sun	*those* girls	*both* ladies
lazy boy	*these* pencils	*all* children

✳ **Colors and numbers are usually adjectives.**

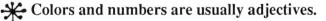

adverb

A word that tells how, when, where, how much, or how often something happens. Adverbs often end in -*ly*. Adverbs describe verbs, adjectives, other adverbs, and sentences.

Examples:

Karen finished her work *quickly*.
He *finally* went home.
Where is my ruler?
Mom was *very* late.
They called home quite *frequently*.
Fortunately, Sam found the key.

almanac

A book published yearly that lists alphabetically a collection of facts, tables, graphs, and information on many subjects and events. Use an almanac for information about:

accidents and disasters	populations
awards	sports records
history and government	weather
music and art	world news

alphabet

The letters of a written language arranged in order.

Examples:

MANUSCRIPT WRITING

Aa Bb Cc Dd Ee Ff Gg Hh Ii Jj Kk Ll Mm
Nn Oo Pp Qq Rr Ss Tt Uu Vv Ww Xx Yy Zz

CURSIVE WRITING

Aa Bb Cc Dd Ee Ff Gg Hh Ii
Jj Kk Ll Mm Nn Oo Pp Qq Rr
Ss Tt Uu Vv Ww Xx Yy Zz

alphabetizing Putting letters or words in alphabetical (A B C) order.

● List by *first* letters all words to be alphabetized.

Examples: apple
banana
coconut

● If all the first letters are the same, alphabetize by the *second* letter.

Examples: pe ach
pl um
pu mpkin

● If the first letter *and* the second letter are the same, alphabetize by the *third* letter.

Examples: pickle
pineapple
pizza

● Use this same method if the first three letters are the same and continue until the letters do not match.

● When alphabetizing people's first and last names, list the *last* name first, followed by a comma, and then write the first name and initial. Then also alphabetize by order of first name.

Examples: Jones, Phillip R.
Jones, Raymond P.
Jones, W.C.

a.m. Ante meridiem; used to show time from after midnight to noon.

Examples: 2:10 a.m. 8:30 a.m. 11:59 a.m.

15

analogy

A comparison between two different words or things that shows how they are alike.

Examples:

Hot is to cold as summer is to winter.
(opposites)

Needle is to sew as pen is to write.
(what the objects are used for)

Finger is to hand as toe is to foot.
(part of a larger thing)

Recognize an analogy by the use of the words "is to" or "is like."

angle [∠]

The space formed when two straight lines touch at the same point.

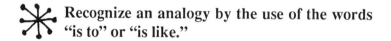

The point is called the vertex, and the lines are called the sides. The symbol for angle is ∠.

When letters are used to name an angle, the vertex (point) is placed between the line (side) letters. The following is angle ∠ BCD:

Angles are measured in degrees (°) with a protractor.

✳ MEASURING HINTS

1. When measuring an angle, remember to measure the space between the lines and not the length of the lines.
2. Line up the center of a protractor (90°) with the vertex of the angle and one side of the angle. Be sure one side of the angle is on the 0° mark.

3. To find the measurement of the angle, read the degrees where the other line of the angle crosses the protractor.

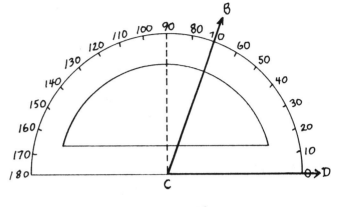

∠ BCD = 70°

✳ HELP

● An **acute angle** is any angle measuring *less* than 90°.

25°

● An **obtuse angle** is any angle measuring *more* than 90°.

120°

● A **right angle** is an angle that measures 90°.

90°

● A **straight angle** measures 180°.

180°

anonymous   Having an unknown name or a name not told or revealed; used when an author's name is not known.

antonym

A word that means the opposite of another word.

> **Examples:** hot .... cold
> love .... hate
> empty .... full
> sweet ..... sour
> win .... lose
> light ...... dark

Also see **synonym.**

**apostrophe
[']**

A punctuation mark used in contractions, posses- sives (words that show ownership), and plurals of numbers, letters, and abbreviations.

CONTRACTIONS

● Use an apostrophe to replace one or more letters or numbers that have been left out.

Examples:

> do not .... don't
> you have ... you've
> 1989 .... '89

POSSESSIVES

● Use an apostrophe to show that an object belongs to someone or something.

Singular Nouns

● Add an apostrophe and *s* to singular nouns.

> **Examples:** Walter's book
> a boy's coat
> one dog's bone

● If a person's name or a word ends in *s,* add an apostrophe and *s.*

Examples: Chris's new car
                waitress's tray

● When two people own one thing, add an apostrophe and *s* to the last name only.

Example:

Larry and Helen's science project
   (one project)

● When two people each own a different thing, add an apostrophe and *s* to both names.

Example:

Larry's and Helen's science projects
   (two projects)

Compound Words
● Add an apostrophe and *s* to the last word of singular compound words.

Examples: everybody else's
                mother-in-law's

Plural Nouns
● Add an apostrophe and *s* to plural nouns *not* ending in *s.*

Examples: children's toys
                deer's antlers
                men's papers

● Add *only* an apostrophe to plural nouns ending with the letter *s.*

Examples: ladie*s*' hats
                boy*s*' houses
                girl*s*' dresses

MORE
→

19

OTHER PLURALS

Add an apostrophe and *s* to a letter, number, or abbreviation to show more than one.

Examples: S O S's

five A's

two 6's

appendix

A section in the back of a book that gives the reader additional useful information the author wishes to include. For example, in a history book, an entire copy of the Mayflower Compact might be included in an appendix:

APPENDIX I

THE MAYFLOWER COMPACT

The threat of James I to "harry them out of the land" sent a little band of religious dissenters from England to Holland in 1608. They were known as "Separatists" because they wished to cut all ties with the Established Church. In 1620, some of them, known now as the Pilgrims, joined with a larger group in England to set sail on the *Mayflower* for the New World. A joint stock company financed their venture.

area

The number of square units inside a shape, such as a rectangle.

● To find the area of a rectangle, multiply the length times the width.

$A = L \times W$

$A = 4' \times 2'$

$A = 8$ feet

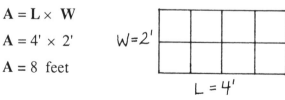

atlas

A book of maps of countries and states. Use an atlas to find information about:

agriculture	language
areas	largest cities
capitals	mountain ranges
currency	populations
flags of countries	religions
important industries	rivers

average

An amount found by adding a group of numbers together and dividing the answer by the number of numerals in the group.

Example: Find the average of 4, 5, and 3.

First, add the numbers together.

$$
\begin{array}{r}
4 \\
5 \\
+3 \\
\hline
12
\end{array}
$$

Then, count the numbers added.

$$
\begin{array}{r}
4 \\
5 \\
+3 \\
\hline
12
\end{array}
$$ 3 numbers

Divide the answer (12) by the number of numerals counted (3).

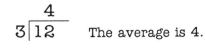

$$
3\overline{)12} \quad \text{The average is 4.}
$$

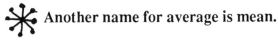 Another name for average is mean.

B

base word   A word without a prefix or a suffix. A base word is sometimes called a root word.

Examples:

Prefix	Base or Root Word	Suffix
un	happy	—
—	pick	ing
dis	appear	ance

B.C.   An abbreviation meaning the time in years before the birth of Christ.

Example:

The date 776 B.C. means seven hundred seventy-six years before the birth of Christ.

Also see **A.D.**

bibliography   A list of books and other written works arranged in alphabetical order by author and found in the back of a text. The materials may have been used by the author and contain more information about topics discussed in the text.

 ✳ **RULES**

- List the author's last name first.
- List the title of the book, magazine, or other publication.
- List where the book or work was published.
- List the publisher.
- List the year of publication.

Example:

Andrews, Ray. *All About Dinasaurs.* New York: Random House, 1963.

Asimov, Isaac. *Did Comets Kill the Dinasaurs?* Milwaukee, Wisc.: Stevens, Inc., 1987.

Beaufay, Gabriel. *Dinasaurs and other Extinct Animals.* New York: Barron Hauppage, 1987.

blend

Two or three consonants sounded together; each one can be heard. A blend is sometimes called a consonant cluster.

Examples:

bl *bl*ock	gl *gl*ad	spr *spr*ing
br *br*ing	gr *gr*ass	st *st*op
cl *cl*ay	pl *pl*an	str *str*eet
cr *cr*eep	pr *pr*ince	sw *sw*ing
dr *dr*ink	sm *sm*all	tr *tr*ain
fl *fl*ag	sn *sn*ap	tw *tw*in
fr *fr*om	sp *sp*ank	

book report

A summarization of the most important events or ideas of a book; also, comments about the book.

❋ HELP

- Tell what kind of story you are reporting about: adventure, humor, mystery, western, historical, or other.
- Tell only the most important ideas or events, not the details.
- Never tell the conclusion of the story.

1. Have you told what kind of story it is and where it takes place?
2. Have you told who the main character is?
3. Have you told what the main character did or needed to do?
4. Have you told what problem the main character had?
5. Have you given a clue to the solution of the problem without telling the ending?
6. Did you like the book?

Example:

Title: *The Story of Ferdinand*

Author: Munro Leaf

Illustrator: Robert Lawson

Main Characters: Ferdinand, his mother, and men from Madrid

Plot Summary: This is an adventure story about Ferdinand, a bull who grew up in Spain. Unlike most bulls who loved to bump heads and fight, Ferdinand liked to sit quietly and smell the flowers. His mother worried about him. One day, because he was the biggest and strongest bull in the pasture, men from Madrid came to the field and took Ferdinand to Madrid to fight in the bull ring. There he had a most unusual experience.

borrowing   In subtraction, the process of exchanging or regrouping numbers to the next smaller place value.

 **✳ HELP**

1. Begin at the ones place; 7 can not be subtracted from 4.

$$\begin{array}{r} 54 \\ -27 \\ \hline \end{array}$$

2. Regroup or exchange 1 ten from the 5 tens for 10 ones.
   Place the 10 ones next to the ones already there.
   10 ones + 4 ones = 14 ones
   Now you can subtract 7 from 14 ones.

$$\begin{array}{r} {}^{4}\cancel{5}4 \\ -27 \\ \hline 7 \end{array}$$

3. Next, subtract 2 tens from the 4 tens.

$$\begin{array}{r} {}^{4}\cancel{5}4 \\ -27 \\ \hline 27 \end{array}$$

✳ MORE HELP

Subtracting from the tens place is done in the same way except you will be exchanging or regrouping from the hundreds place.

1. Take 1 hundred from the 7 hundreds and exchange it for 10 tens.
2. Place the 10 tens next to the 2 tens.
   10 tens + 2 tens = 12 tens
3. Now you can subtract 4 tens from 12 tens.

$$\begin{array}{r} {}^{6}\cancel{7}\cancel{2}6 \\ -342 \\ \hline 84 \end{array}$$

MORE →

borrowing, cont.

4. To finish the problem, subtract 3 hundreds from the 6 hundreds.

$$
\begin{array}{r}
\cancel{7}\cancel{2}6 \\
-342 \\
\hline
384
\end{array}
$$

C

calendar   A chart showing the days, weeks, and months of a year.

DAYS OF THE WEEK
There are seven days in a week.

Day	Abbreviation
Sunday	Sun.
Monday	Mon.
Tuesday	Tues.
Wednesday	Wed.
Thursday	Thurs.
Friday	Fri.
Saturday	Sat.

MONTHS
There are twelve months in a year.

Month	Abbreviation	Days
January	Jan.	31
February	Feb.	28 (29 in a leap year)
March	Mar.	31
April	Apr.	30
May	May	31
June	June	30
July	July	31
August	Aug.	31
September	Sept.	30
October	Oct.	31
November	Nov.	30
December	Dec.	31

MORE →

An easy way to remember the number of days in each month:

1. Make a fist.

2. Touch your first knuckle and call it "January." It has 31 days.

3. Touch the space between your first knuckle and second knuckle. Call this "February." It has 28 days.

4. While saying the months of the year in order, every "knuckle month" will have 31 days. Every "space" month will have 30 days, except February, which has 28.

5. Repeat, beginning with "August" on your first knuckle.

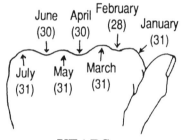

YEARS

365 days	=	1 year
366 days	=	1 leap year *
52 weeks	=	1 year
12 months	=	1 year
10 years	=	1 decade
100 years	=	1 century

*A leap year occurs every four years; 1988 was a leap year.

How to write the date:

November 12, 1990
Nov. 12, 1990
11/12/90

capital letter   A letter written or printed in a larger size and sometimes in a different form from its corresponding, smaller, lower-case version.

 **RULES**

● Capitalize the first word in a sentence.

Example: Please feed the baby.

● Capitalize the first word in every line of poetry.

Examples:

A new capital every time
You begin a new line of rhyme.

● Capitalize the first word in a direct quotation.

Examples:

The clown asked, "Are you having fun?"
"Yes, I am," answered the boy.

● Capitalize the names of persons and their initials.

Examples: James Tyler Smith
J.T. Smith
Patricia R. Penny
P.R. Penny

● Capitalize titles of persons when they come before people's names.

Examples: President Wilson
Captain Anderson
Senator Lawton
Bishop Cartwright

 Do not capitalize titles that follow names.

Examples:

John Anderson, a captain in the Marines.
Mary Clark, president of CRC.

● Capitalize abbreviations of titles and names.

Examples: Dr. Black

Gen. McArthur

Sam Standish, Sr.

John Johnson, Jr.

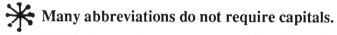 **Many abbreviations do not require capitals.**

Examples: doz., in., ft. yd., vol.

● Capitalize words that show a family relationship when they are used as names or with the person's given name.

Examples:

Will Mother be late, Sis?

I wrote a note to Aunt Marcy.

But: My mother is late.

● Capitalize days of the week, months of the year, and holidays.

Examples: Monday, Tuesday

January, February

Halloween, Christmas

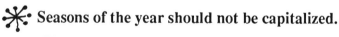 **Seasons of the year should not be capitalized.**

Examples: spring, summer, fall, winter.

● Capitalize the first word and all important words in the greeting of a letter.

Examples: Hi, Dad,

Dear Aunt Jo and Uncle Cal,

● Capitalize only the first word in the closing of a letter.

Examples: Sincerely yours,

Very truly yours,

Your friend,

● Capitalize names of races, nationalities, tribes, languages, and religions.

> **Examples:** Apache
> French
> German
> Jewish

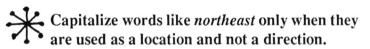 **Do not capitalize words based on size or color.**

> **Examples:** white, black, red man.

● Capitalize words naming special places.

> **Examples:** Grand Canyon
> South Dakota
> Atlantic Ocean
> the Northeast

Capitalize words like *northeast* only when they are used as a location and not a direction.

> **Examples:**
> Andy lives in the Northeast. (location)
> Amy traveled northeast. (direction)

● Capitalize names of organizations and businesses.

> **Examples:** the Democratic Party
> Chicago Symphony
> Boy Scouts
> the Ford Motor Company

● Capitalize names of school subjects that are names of languages or used as titles.

> **Examples:** English
> Latin
> Spelling
> Algebra

MORE
→

31

Names of school subjects used as part of a sentence are not capitalized unless they are names of languages.

Examples:
Lola has gym at 11 o'clock.
Sandy is studying French.

● Capitalize the first and important words in titles of books, magazines, newspapers, or other works.

Examples: The Chicago Tribune
The Case of the Lost Jewel

 Do not capitalize small words within a title like *in, the, a, and.*

● Capitalize names of historic events and documents.

Examples: the Bill of Rights
the Civil War

● Capitalize abbreviations for time in history, organizations, businesses, and departments in government.

A.D.	IRS
B.C.	WW II
CBS	NATO
IBM	YMCA

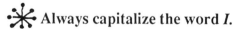 Always capitalize the word *I.*

Examples:
I finished my work.
When I finish, I can go swimming.

cardinal number

A number that shows *how many.*

Examples: 429, 1, 23

Also see **ordinal number.**

casting out nines

A method of checking the accuracy of an addition, subtraction, multiplication, or division problem.

ADDITION

Add across each row of addends, subtracting any total of 9 until you end with a digit less than 9.

Example: **end digits**

$$236 \quad = 2 + 3 + 6 = 11 - 9 = 2$$
$$327 \quad = 3 + 2 + 7 = 12 - 9 = 3$$
$$\underline{+158} \quad = 1 + 5 + 8 = 14 - 9 = 5$$
$$721$$

Add the end digits and subtract 9 from the total.

$$2$$
$$3$$
$$\underline{+5}$$
$$10 - 9 = \boxed{1}$$

Add the numbers in the sum; subtract any total of 9.

$$721 = 7 + 2 + 1 = 10 - 9 = \boxed{1}$$

When each casting out process ends up with the same number, the problem has been added correctly.

SUBTRACTION

The same process is used in casting out nines in subtraction as in addition except that the end digits are subtracted.

Example:

                                         end digits

$$756 \quad = 7 + 5 + 6 = 18 - 9 = \quad 9$$
$$\underline{-29} \quad = 2 + 9 \quad\quad = 11 - 9 = \underline{-2}$$
$$727 \quad\quad\quad\quad\quad\quad\quad\quad\quad\quad \boxed{7}$$

$$727 = 7 + 2 + 7 = 16 - 9 = \boxed{7}$$

MORE →

MULTIPLICATION

The same process is used except that the two end digits are multiplied.

Example: **end digits**

$$463 = 4 + 6 + 3 = 13 - 9 = 4$$
$$\underline{\times 37} = 3 + 7 \qquad = 10 - 9 = \underline{\times 1}$$
$$3241 \qquad\qquad\qquad\qquad\qquad 4$$
$$\underline{1389}$$
$$17131 = 1 + 7 + 1 + 3 + 1 = 13 - 9 = 4$$

LONG DIVISION

Divide the problem in the usual way.

Example:

```
        28
    24|672
       48
       192
       192
```

Then, follow these steps to check your answer:

Multiply the quotient by the divisor.

```
        28
       ×24
       112
        56
       672
```

Cast out nines as in multiplication problems.

end digits

$$
\begin{array}{rcll}
28 &=& 2 + 8 = 10 - 9 &= \quad 1 \\
\times\,24 &=& 2 + 4 = \quad 6 &= \quad \times 6 \\
\hline
112 & & & \quad \enclose{circle}{6} \\
56 & & & \\
\hline
672 &=& 6 + 7 + 2 = 15 - 9 &= \enclose{circle}{6}
\end{array}
$$

Celsius thermometer

A metric thermometer named for its inventor, Anders Celsius. On the Celsius thermometer scale, 0 degrees is the temperature at which water freezes, and 100 degrees is the temperature at which water boils.

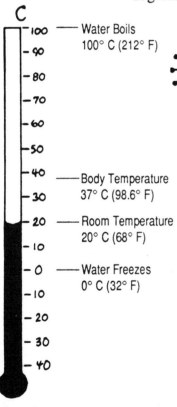

❋ The temperature 8° C is read "eight degrees Celsius."

To convert a Celsius temperature to a Fahrenheit temperature, multiply the Celsius temperature by $\frac{9}{5}$ and add 32.

Formula:

Celsius temp. $\times \frac{9}{5} + 32° =$ Fahrenheit temp.

Example:

$10°C \times \frac{9}{5} = 18 + 32° = 50°F$

Also see **Fahrenheit thermometer.**

centimeter

A unit of length in the metric system equal to $\frac{1}{100}$ of a meter. Use a centimeter ruler to measure short lengths.

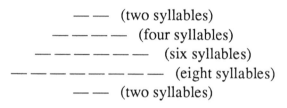

❋ RULES

10 millimeters (mm)	=	1 centimeter (cm)
10 centimeters (cm)	=	1 decimeter (dm)
100 millimeters (mm)	=	1 decimeter (dm)
10 decimeters (dm)	=	1 meter (m)
100 centimeters (cm)	=	1 meter (m)
1000 meters (m)	=	1 kilometer (km)

Also see **measurement chart.**

cinquain

A five-line stanza with a definite number of syllables in each line. Invented by Adelaide Crapsey who was greatly influenced by the Japanese haiku.

— — (two syllables)
— — — — (four syllables)
— — — — — — (six syllables)
— — — — — — — — (eight syllables)
— — (two syllables)

Example:

Kitten
Soft and fluffy
Sleeps, yawns, stretches, and purrs
Makes me feel warm, cozy, happy
Nice pet.

circle

See **geometric figures.**

circumference

The curved line of a circle; the length around a circle.

The circumference of a circle is a little more than three times its diameter. (The diameter is a straight line through the center of the circle from one point on the circle to another point on the circle.)

✳ RULES

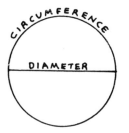

To find the circumference of a circle:
- Measure the diameter.
- Multiply the diameter by 3.14 (which is pi).
- Or for a quick estimate of a circumference, multiply the diameter by 3.

> **Example:**   Diameter = 4 inches
>   Then 4 × 3 = 12
>
> The circumference measures about 12 inches.

Also see **diameter** and **pi**.

clause

A group of words containing a verb (action word) and a subject. A clause may be a complete sentence or may be part of a sentence.

> **Examples:**
>
> I ducked *when Jan threw the ball.*
>
> It rained hard, *but the river did not overflow.*
>
> *The dog barked.*

colon [:]

A punctuation mark used to introduce an explanation or a list. A colon is also used with numerals to show time and in the greeting of a business letter.

> **Examples:**
>
> The color of her dress is violet: a beautiful bluish purple. (explanation)
>
> Please bring the following items to class: pencils, paper, and rulers. (list)
>
> 3:20 p.m. (numerals; time)
>
> Dear Sir: (greeting)
>
> Dear Mrs. Blake: (greeting)

37

comma [,]   A punctuation mark placed where a pause in speaking would be made.

 **✳RULES**

- **Address** Use a comma as part of an address.

  Examples:
  Her address is 123 Oak Street, Chicago, Illinois.
  Tom lives on Rural Route 2, Ames, Iowa.
  You can send Jane's letter to Apt. 728, 114 Elm Street, Dallas, Texas.
  Send your request to Box 123, Cleveland, Ohio.

- **City in State or Country** Use a comma to separate the name of a city from a state or country.

  Examples:
  Kevin lives in Arlington, Virginia.
  London, England, is an important city in Europe.
  We visited Disney World in Orlando, Florida.

- **Conjunctions** Use a comma between two independent clauses joined by the conjunctions *and, but, or, for, nor, so,* or *yet.*

  Examples:
  Tom hit a long fly ball, and Joe scored the winning run.
  It rained all day, but the ballgame was played.
  Help me with this work, or I'll never finish.

- **Conjunctive Adverbs** Use a comma after conjunctive adverbs such as *however, nevertheless, therefore,* and *furthermore.*

  Example:
  I read the book; *however,* I didn't like the ending.

- **Dates** Use a comma after parts of a date.

  Examples:
  She was born on July 28, 1988.
  We moved to Dallas on May 11, 1983.
  School began on September 5, 1986, and
   ended on June 10, 1987.
  Today is Tuesday, January 30, 1990.

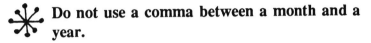 **Do not use a comma between a month and a year.**

  Example: December 1899.

- **Direct Address** Use a comma when you are speaking directly to someone.

  Examples:
  Sandy, please help me.
  What will you wear to the dance, Sally?
  Hurry, Sue, or we'll be late.
  Laura Jane, will you bake some cookies?

- **Direct Quotation** Use a comma before or after a direct quotation.

  Examples:
  "Mom, I won the race," called Andy.
  Donna sighed, "I have to clean my room."

- **Letters** Use a comma after the greeting of a friendly letter.

  Examples: Dear Tina,
   Dear Mr. Smith,

  Also use a comma after the closing of all letters.

  Examples: Your friend,
   Sincerely yours,

● **Parenthetical Expressions**   Use a comma before and after parenthetical expressions such as *by the way, for example,* or *on the other hand.*

Example:

The baseball team, *for example,* always rides in a special bus.

● **Series**   Use a comma to separate items in a list of things in a sentence.

Examples:

Paul enjoys watching baseball, football, and tennis.

The winning numbers were 43, 2, 70, and 100.

I looked for my keys under the bed, in the drawer, and in my purse.

When boating, wear a life jacket, carry a flashlight, take fresh water, and stay with your group.

● **Too**   Use a comma to separate the word *too* in a sentence.

Examples:

Phil likes to play tennis, too.

August, too, is a hot month.

● **Yes, No, Well, Oh**   Use a comma after *yes, no, well,* and *oh* when they begin sentences.

Examples:

Yes, I'll be ready at noon.

No, lunch isn't ready.

Well, what will we do now?

Oh, I can't wait for the circus to come!

compass rose

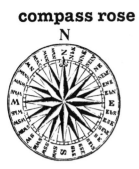

A symbol printed on a chart or map to show the points of a compass, numbered from true north and showing 360°.

● Memorizing "Never Eat Soggy Waffles" (North) (East) (South) (West) will help you to remember the directions in order.

compound sentence

A sentence with two or more complete thoughts joined together by words that connect (*and, but, or, nor, for, yet,* and *so*).

Example:

Tim came early, and *we went to the zoo.*

Each complete thought could be a sentence by itself.

compound word

Two words combined or put together to form one word.

Examples: butter fly   butterfly

play ground   playground

COMMON COMPOUND WORDS

anyone	headline	quarterback
blackboard	indoor	railroad
classroom	lightweight	sidewalk
downstairs	mailman	themselves
everywhere	northeast	underwear
flashlight	outdoors	weekend
grandfather	paperback	yourself

✳ **Common compound words that need hyphens:**

cave-in	flea-bitten	jack-in-the-box
drive-in	forget-me-not	up-to-date

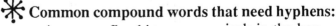

address a different letter or number to tell a computer where to find information.

Basic a simple computer programming language.

binary code a system using only 1 and 0 in different combinations to represent letters, numbers, and characters.

bug an error or problem in a computer program.

command an order telling a computer what to do; given by pressing the proper key on the keyboard.

computer a piece of hardware that takes in information, processess and stores it, and prints out information.

CPU Central Processing Unit: the control center of a computer.

cursor a symbol that shows where the next letter, number, or marking will appear on the video screen.

data information given to, stored in, or processed by a computer.

data bank information stored in a computer's memory.

disk a round device similar to a record used to store large amounts of information to be used by a computer.

hardware computer equipment including the keyboard, video monitor, printer, disks, and tapes.

input data given to a computer.

keyboard a set of keys similar to those found on a typewriter used to type information into a computer.

loop a part of a computer program that repeats.

memory an area within a computer in which information is stored.

menu a screen display listing programs in the computer.

printer a piece of hardware that prints out information from a computer.

program instructions coded to tell a computer what to do.

RAM Random Access Memory, where information is stored in the computer temporarily and where information can be written or read before it is saved on a disk.

ROM Read Only Memory, where information is stored in a computer on a permanent basis.

run a command that tells a computer to run a program it has stored in its memory.

software a variety of computer programs.

VDU Visual Display Unit, the screen used to display computer information.

word processor software that allows the user to type, edit, and finalize articles, books, and written work on an automatic typewriter or on a computer.

congruent

Having the same size and shape.

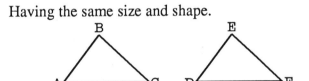

Triangles ABC and DEF are congruent triangles.

conjunction

A word that connects two or more independent clauses or complete thoughts.

Examples:

Dad will come to the ballgame, *but* he may be late.

Also see **comma.**

43

consonant

Any letter of the alphabet that is not a vowel:

b c d f g h j k l m n p q r s t v w x y z

**consonant
cluster**

See **blend**.

continent

One of seven land masses of the earth: Africa, Antarctica, Asia, Australia, Europe, North America, and South America.

Also see **map of continents** on the next page.

contraction

A shortened form of two words. In a contraction, one or more letters are omitted in making the new word, and an apostrophe (') is used in place of the letter or letters that were dropped.

COMMON CONTRACTIONS

I am ....I'm	is not ....isn't
you are ....you're	are not ....aren't
it is ....it's	was not ....wasn't
they are ....they're	were not ....weren't
I have ....I've	has not ....hasn't
they have ....they've	have not ....haven't
I had ....I'd	cannot ....can't
I will ....I'll	will not ....won't
we will ....we'll	does not ....doesn't
I would ....I'd	do not ....don't
here is ....here's	did not ....didn't
there is ....there's	would not ....wouldn't
who is ....who's	should not ....shouldn't

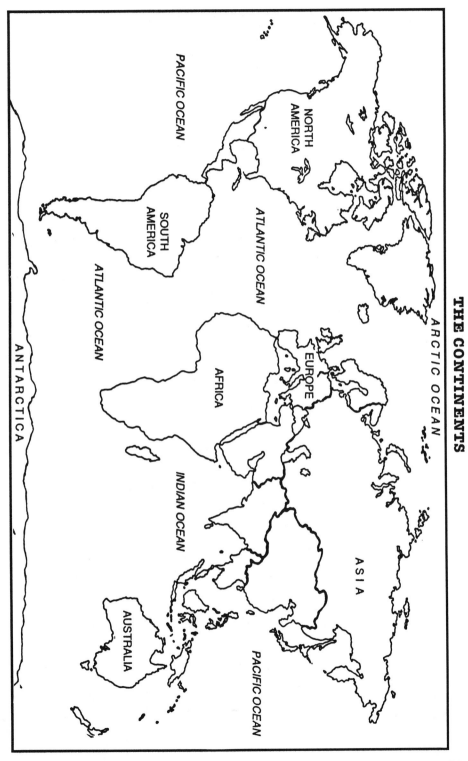

THE CONTINENTS

45

days of the week

See **calendar.**

decimal

Any base-ten numeral that uses place value to represent a number. The position of the decimal point (written as a dot) determines the value of each number.

- Numbers to the left of a decimal point are whole numbers called integers.

  Examples:

  The number 7.0 is read "seven."
  The number 48.0 is read "forty-eight."

- Numbers to the right of a decimal point are decimal fractions. Their value is less than one.

  Examples:

  The number 0.5 is read "five-tenths."
  The number 48.5 is read "forty-eight and five-tenths."

Also see **decimal chart** on the next page and **percent.**

declarative sentence

See **sentence.**

DECIMAL CHART

100,000,000	10,000	1,000	100	10	1	.	$\frac{1}{10}$	$\frac{1}{100}$	$\frac{1}{1,000}$	$\frac{1}{10,000}$	$\frac{1}{100,000}$	$\frac{1}{1,000,000,000}$
hundred thousands	ten thousands	thousands	hundreds	tens	ones	decimal point	tenths	hundredths	thousandths	ten-thousandths	hundred-thousandths	millionths

PLACE OF DIGIT	HOW TO WRITE IT	HOW TO READ IT	FRACTION
First decimal place	.3	Three tenths..............................	$\frac{3}{10}$
Second decimal place	.03	Three hundredths	$\frac{3}{100}$
Third decimal place..........	.003	Three thousandths	$\frac{3}{1000}$
Fourth decimal place	.0003	Three ten-thousandths.............	$\frac{3}{10,000}$
Fifth decimal place	.00003	Three hundred-thousandths.......	$\frac{3}{100,000}$
Sixth decimal place	.000003	Three millionths	$\frac{3}{1,000,000,000}$

Example: 502.062 is read "five hundred two <u>and</u> sixty-two thousandths."

degree
[°]

A unit of measurement for angles or temperature.

Also see **angle, Celsius thermometer, circle,** and
Fahrenheit thermometer.

denominator

The number in the bottom of a fraction. The denominator tells how many equal parts there are in all.

Example:

$$\frac{1}{8}$$ The number 8 is the
denominator.

Also see **fraction** and **numerator.**

Dewey
decimal
system

A way of organizing and numbering nonfiction books
under 10 subject areas developed by Melvil Dewey.

000-099	Generalities
100-199	Philosophy and Related Disciplines
200-299	Religion
300-399	Social Sciences
400-499	Language
500-599	Sciences
600-699	Technology and Applied Sciences
700-799	Fine Arts
800-899	Literature
900-999	History and Geography

diagram

A drawing or sketch showing the important parts of
an object or how something works.

Examples:

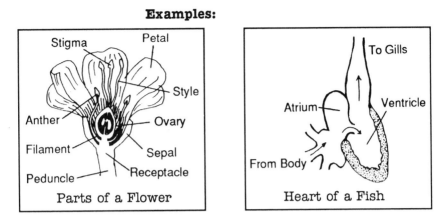

Parts of a Flower

Heart of a Fish

diameter   A straight line through the center of a circle from one point on the circle to another point. The diameter can travel in any direction as long as it passes through the center of the circle.

Examples:

Also see **circumference** and **pi.**

dictionary   A reference book that lists words alphabetically and explains the meaning, pronunciation, and part of speech of each word. Dictionaries may also include synonyms, antonyms, and biographical and geographic listings.

49

Examples:

A

az‑ure (azh′ər) adj. Of or like the color of a clear sky.

az‑u‑rite (azh′ ə-rīt) n. A brilliantly blue, monoclinic material.

B

B, b (bē) n. The second letter of the English alphabet: from the Greek *beta.*

baa (bă) n. The cry of a sheep or goat.

difference

The answer to a subtraction problem.

Also see **subtraction.**

digraph

See **vowel digraph.**

dividend

A number to be divided by another number.

Example:

$$3\overline{)9}$$ The number 9 is the dividend.

division

A way of finding out how many groups of one number can be found in another number.

Example:

$$15 \div 5 \quad \text{or} \quad 5\overline{)15}$$

In the number 15, there are 3 groups of 5.

Because division is the reverse of multiplication, think of a multiplication fact that will equal the dividend.

Example:

$$5 \times 3 = 15 \quad \text{so} \quad 5\overline{)15}^{\,3}$$

LONG DIVISION

To remember the steps used in long division, think of this saying:

Do   Monkeys   Sleep   Bare?

$$3\overline{)48}$$

Do (Divide): How many groups of 3 are in 4? (1)
Monkeys (Multiply): $1 \times 3 = 3$
Sleep (Subtract): $4 - 3 = 1$
Bare (Bring down): Bring down the number 8 next.

$$
\begin{array}{r}
1 \\
3\overline{)48} \\
\underline{3} \\
18
\end{array}
$$

Begin again with **Do** (Divide) and continue until there are no more numbers to bring down. What is left is called the *remainder*. There are 16 groups of 3 in 48.

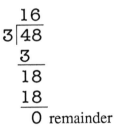

$$
\begin{array}{r}
16 \\
3\overline{)48} \\
\underline{3} \\
18 \\
\underline{18} \\
0 \text{ remainder}
\end{array}
$$

Also see **casting out nines** and **remainder.**

divisor   A number by which another number is to be divided.

Example:

$2\overline{)36}$ The number 2 is the divisor.

E

edit

To review the content and organization of a written work, revise as necessary, and correct errors in grammar, spelling, and punctuation.

Also see **proofreading symbols.**

ellipsis
[. . .]

A series of three dots used to show that a word or words were omitted from a sentence or that someone's statement was interrupted.

Examples:
An apple a day . . . away. (omission)
"How much is . . . Hey! What's going on here?" (interruption)

encyclopedia

A book or set of books that contains information on many subjects. The subjects are listed alphabetically.

equator

An imaginary circle around the middle of the earth, halfway between the North Pole and the South Pole. The equator is 0° latitude.

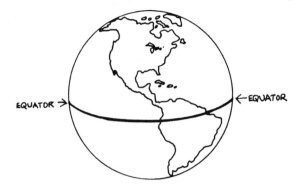

Also see **latitude.**

equivalent

Equal; having equal value.

Examples:
One nickel is equivalent to 5 cents.

The fraction $\frac{2}{4}$ is equivalent to $\frac{1}{2}$.

Also see **percent.**

essay

A short piece of writing; a composition expressing the author's opinion.

estimate

To figure approximately; to form an opinion or judgment. Not exact.

Examples:

Jim estimated that 37 and 22 are about 60.
Our books will be delivered in about one
week.
I think the battery will cost about $90.00
plus tax.

Also see **rounding.**

exclamation point [!]

A punctuation mark used after a word or sentence to give a sharp command or to show surprise, joy, fear, shock, or other strong emotion.

Examples:

Help! Watch out! Stop!
What a wonderful day!
There's a tornado!

exclamatory sentence

See sentence.

expanded numeral

A numeral written in expanded notation; a method of showing the value named by each digit in a numeral.

Example: $5,207 = 5,000$
200
00
7

or $5,207 = 5000 + 200 + 00 + 7$

exponent

A numeral written slightly above and to the right of a number to tell how many times that number is to be used as a factor.

Example:

In the number 10^3, the numeral 3 is the exponent. It shows that 10 is used as a factor, a number to be multiplied, 3 times.

$$10^3 = 10 \times 10 \times 10 \text{ or } 1,000$$

F

fact or opinion

A *fact* is a true statement; it can be proven.

Example:

There are 12 months in a year.

An *opinion* tells how someone feels or thinks about something.

Example:

April is the best month of the year.

factor

A number to be multiplied by another number.

Example:

The numbers 2 and 4 are factors.

Fahrenheit thermometer

A thermometer that has a temperature scale on which 32° is the freezing point of water and 212° the boiling point. The Fahrenheit thermometer was named for Gabriel D. Fahrenheit.

✳ The temperature 80°F is read "eighty degrees Fahrenheit."

55

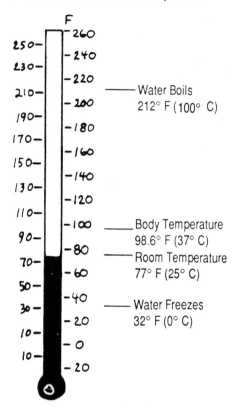

To convert Fahrenheit temperature to Celsius, subtract 32 from the Fahrenheit temperature and multiply the remainder by $\frac{5}{9}$.

Formula:
Fahrenheit temp. $- 32° \times \frac{5}{9}$
= Celsius temp.

Example:
$86°F - 32 = 54 \times \frac{5}{9} = 30°C$

Also see **Celsius thermometer.**

fiction

Imaginative writings including stories, plays, and poems.

Examples:
Alice in Wonderland by Lewis B. Carroll
Moby Dick by Herman Melville

fraction

Two numbers separated by a line. The number above the line is called the *numerator*; the number below the line is called the *denominator*. A fraction tells the number of parts of a whole.

Examples:

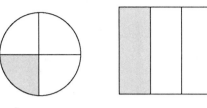

$\frac{1}{4}$ means 1 part of 4 equal parts (the whole).

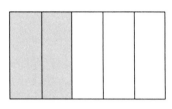

$\frac{2}{5}$ means 2 parts of 5 equal parts (the whole).

In the illustration, $\frac{3}{5}$ of the figures have flags.

Also see **denominator, equivalent,** and **numerator.**

fraction number line

A number line that shows fractions in order from the smallest to the greatest.

0    $\frac{1}{8}$ $\frac{1}{4}$ $\frac{3}{8}$ $\frac{1}{2}$ $\frac{5}{8}$ $\frac{3}{4}$ $\frac{7}{8}$ 1

geographic terms   Terms used in the study of geography.

COMMON GEOGRAPHIC TERMS

archipelago A sea with a large group of islands.

bay Part of the sea that extends into the land.

butte A hill that rises sharply and has a flat top.

canyon A narrow valley with high steep walls; a gorge.

cape A point of land that juts out into a body of water.

channel A deep part of a river or harbor.

delta An area of land shaped like a triangle in which sand and dirt collect at the mouth of a river.

desert A dry area having little vegetation or water.

dune A ridge or hill of sand heaped up by the wind.

fjord A long, narrow inlet of the sea between high cliffs.

glacier A large mass of ice that moves slowly down a mountain.

gulf A large part of an ocean or sea partly surrounded by land.

horizon The line along which the land and sky appear to meet.

island Land, smaller than a continent, entirely surrounded by water.

isthmus A narrow strip of land that runs between two bodies of water and joins two bodies of land.

lake A large body of salt or fresh water surrounded by land.

levee A bank built along a river to keep it from flooding.

mesa A hill with one or more steep sides and a flat top, common in very dry areas.

mountain A very high elevation in the earth's surface, usually with steep sides.

oasis A fertile area with water located in a desert.

peninsula A piece of land that projects out into the water from a larger land mass.

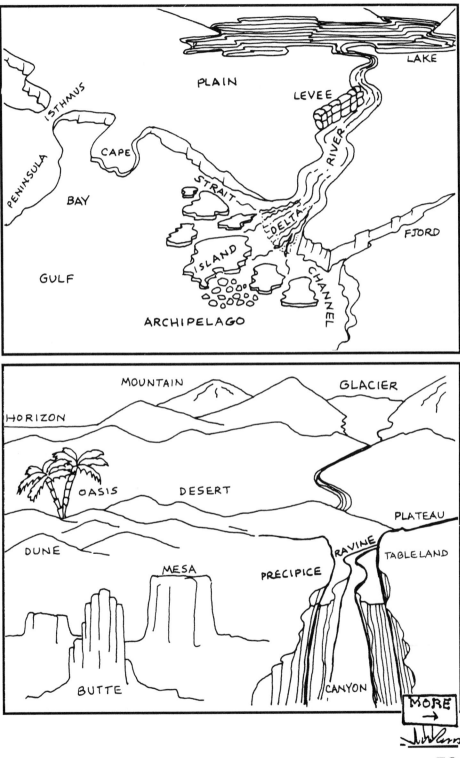

---

plain A flat stretch of land.
plateau A plain; level land usually higher than land around it.
precipice A very steep or overhanging mass of rock; a cliff.
ravine A deep, narrow gorge, usually made by running water.
strait A narrow channel connecting two larger bodies of water.
tableland A high plain; plateau; mesa.

---

geography   The study of the earth's surface, continents, climate, peoples, governments, industries, and products.

geometric figures   Figures formed from straight lines or curved lines.

COMMON GEOMETRIC FIGURES

circle A closed curve with all points an equal distance from the center. There are 360° in a circle.

cone A solid figure with a flat, round base at one end and that tapers to a point at the opposite end.

cube A solid figure with 6 square faces of equal size.

cylinder A solid figure with 2 round ends of equal size.

hexagon A figure with 6 straight sides and 6 angles; a polygon.

octagon A figure with 8 straight sides and 8 angles; a polygon

---

parallelogram A figure with opposite sides parallel; a quadrilateral.

 pentagon A figure with 5 straight sides and 5 angles; a polygon.

 polygon A closed figure with line segments as sides.

 prism A solid figure with 2 equal bases. A prism is named for the shape of its bases.

 quadrilateral A figure with 4 straight sides and 4 angles.

 rectangle A four-sided figure with 4 right angles.

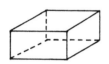 **rectangular prism** A solid figure with 2 parallel rectangular bases and 4 faces that are parallelograms.

 rhombus A parallelogram that has all sides equal.

 square A rectangle that has all sides equal and 4 right angles. A square is also a rhombus.

 trapezoid A figure that has only 2 sides parallel.

 triangle A polygon with 3 straight sides.

 triangular prism A solid figure with 2 triangular bases and 3 rectangular faces.

glossary   A list of difficult, special, or unusual words with their meanings, usually placed at the back of a book.

Example:

archeologist   a scientist who studies archeology

basalt   dark, volcanic rock

chisel   a cutting tool for engraving on metal, stone, or wood.

Dead Sea   a salt lake on the Israel-Jordan border

graph   A drawing that shows the relationship between different kinds of information.

SOME KINDS OF GRAPHS

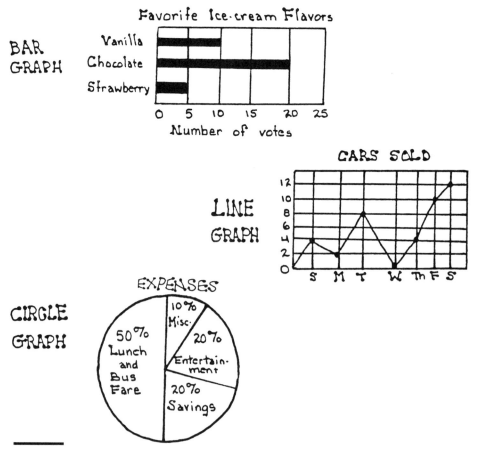

62

Great Lakes   Five large lakes in the United States. Four (Lake Huron, Lake Ontario, Lake Erie, and Lake Superior) lie between the United States and Canada. Lake Michigan lies within the United States.

An easy way to remember the names of the great lakes: Think of the word **H O M E S.**

H	Huron
O	Ontario
M	Michigan
E	Erie
S	Superior

Also see **United States of America map.**

greater than   [>]   A term and symbol used to compare two numbers. The widest part of the symbol faces the larger number.

Examples:

10 > 5   The number 10 is greater than 5.

400 > 200   The number 400 is greater than 200.

grid   A pattern of horizontal and vertical lines spaced to form squares of equal size. Grids are used on maps to locate places and in math to locate numbers.

Los Angeles, Denver and Miami can be found in the grid on the next page.

grid, cont.

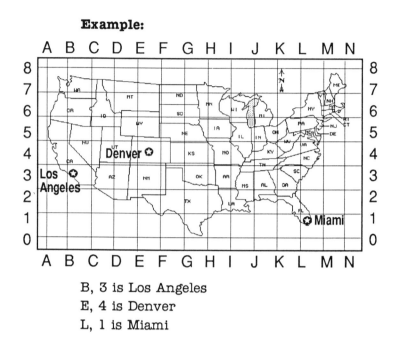

B, 3 is Los Angeles
E, 4 is Denver
L, 1 is Miami

※ **Always locate a point by moving to the right first and then up.**

Also see **multiplication table.**

guide words   Words printed in dark lettering at the top of each page of a dictionary or reference book. Guide words tell the first and last words printed on the page.

To find if a word is listed on a page or comes before or after that page, follow these examples.
For instance, to find the word *boom:*

1. Line up the letters of *boot*, the *first* guide word and *boom*, the word you are checking. Find the first pair of letters that are different.

boot / **bottom**   (guide words)
boom

64

boot / bottom

boot (boot), *n.* 1, an outer covering for the foot, usually of leather, coming above the ankle: a high shoe; 2, especially, in the United States, such a covering, either of leather or of rubber, and reaching either the knee or the hip; 3, a place for baggage in a coach, carriage, or automobile:—*v.t.,* 1, to put boots on (someone); 2, to kick.
booth (booth; booth), *n.* 1, a temporary stall for the sale of goods, for a puppet show, or the like; 2, an enclosure to ensure privacy.
boot-leg-ger (boot leg ger), *Slang, n.* one who makes or sells something, especially alcoholic liquors, in violation of the law.—*v.t., v.i.,* and *adj.* boot leg .—*n.* boot leg ging.
boot-y (boo ti), *n.* [*pl.* booties], 1, food, guns, and the like, taken from the enemy in war; 2, the plunder of thieves and robbers; 3, any rich prize or gain.
bor-ax (bor aks), *n.* a white crystalline compound of sodium, boron, and oxygen: used as a cleaning agent or antiseptic.
bor-der (bor der), *n.* 1, the edge of anything, as of a lake; 2, a boundary or frontier, as of a country; 3, a narrow strip along

or around something; as a handkerchief with a lace *border.*
bore (bor), *v.t.* [bored, bor-ing], to weary by tiresome repetition or dullness.
bor-ough (bur o) *n.* an incorporated town; also in England, a town represented in parliament.
bor-row (bor o), *v.t.* 1, to obtain something with the understanding that is is to be returned; 2, to copy; adopt.
boss (bos), *Colloquial, n.* 1, a superintendent of workmen; a foreman; also an employer; 2, a politician who controls a large number of votes.
both (both), *adj.* the one and the other; not one only. but two; as, both boys were *lost.*
bot-tle (bot l), *n.* 1, a narrow-necked vessel without handles, usually of glass; 2, the contents of such a vessel.
bot-tom (bot um), *n.* 1, the lowest part of anything, as of a hill; 2, the part underneath; the base, as of a barrel; 3, the basis, the essential point.

2. Does the letter *m* in the word *boom* come before or after *t* in the guide word *boot?*

3. If you answered "before," the word you are comparing will not be found on this page but on a page *before* it.

4. Now look for the word *both.* The letter *t* comes *after o* in the guide word, *boot.*

Continue to compare *both* in the same way with *bottom,* the second guide word.

bo*o*t / bo*t*tom
b*o*th bo*th*

5. The letter *h* in *both* comes before the *t* in *bottom,* the second guide word. The word *both* will be found *on* this page.

6. Look for the word *box.*

bo*o*t / bo*t*tom
b*o*x b*o*x

In this case, the letter *x* in *box* comes *after* the *o* in *boot* and *after* the *t* in *bottom.* The word *box* will be found on a page *after* this page.

H

haiku

An unrhymed poem that has three lines with five syllables in the first line, seven syllables in the second, and five syllables in the third line. The poem contains only 17 syllables.

Example:

Swift, flying eagle,   1st line, 5 syllables

Soaring high among the clouds 2nd line, 7 syllables

Lost in his own thoughts.   3rd line, 5 syllables

hemisphere

Half of a globe or sphere; the northern and southern hemispheres of the earth, as divided by the equator, or the eastern and western hemispheres of the earth, as divided by the Prime Meridian.

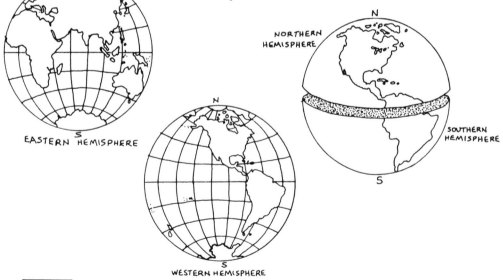

EASTERN HEMISPHERE

WESTERN HEMISPHERE

NORTHERN HEMISPHERE

SOUTHERN HEMISPHERE

homograph

One of two or more words that are spelled the same but have different meanings, origins, and sometimes different sounds.

Examples:

wound   Tom wound the clock.

wound   Bandage the wound.

homonym

One of two or more words that have the same sound and usually the same spelling but have different meanings.

Examples:

saw   I saw him yesterday.

saw   Gerry can saw wood.

homophone

One of two or more words that sound alike but have different meanings, origins, and usually different spellings.

Examples:

wait   Wait for me!

weight   Watch your weight.

horizontal line

A straight line, usually drawn from left to right, parallel to the plane of the horizon and level ground.

Example:

_____

hyphen [-]

A punctuation mark used to join the parts of a compound word or to follow the first part of a word divided at the end of a line.

✳ RULES

● Use a hyphen to join some compound words.

Examples: self-control   fifty-one

one-half   sister-in-law

drive-in   vice-president

● Use a hyphen when two or more words are used as an adjective and come before the word they modify.

Example:

That was a fast-paced race.

Exception: Do not use a hyphen with an adverb ending in -*ly* used with an adjective or a participle.

Example: She will not buy a poorly built car.

● Use a hyphen to divide a word at the end of a line.

Example:

Jan and I are going to divide that piece of cake.

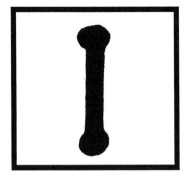

I and me

When *I* or *me* is used with a noun or another pronoun, be polite; use *I* or *me* last.

Examples:
Cissy and *I* love pizza. (with a noun)
You and *I* can share these crayons. (with a pronoun)
The baby laughed at Steve and *me*.
The dog followed her and *me*.

● To decide whether to use *I* or *me* in a sentence, cover the noun or other pronoun and decide if the sentence is correct.

Examples:
Barbara and me went to the movies.
Barbara and I went to the movies.

Cover up *Barbara* and read the first sentence. "Me went to the movies" is not correct. "I went to the movies" is correct.

idiom

An expression or saying with words that are not meant literally but which have a special meaning. The words say one thing but mean another.

idiom, cont.

Examples:

"You *put your foot in your mouth*" means
you said something you shouldn't have.

"Sarah is *sitting on top of the world*" means
Sarah is feeling extremely happy.

imperative   *See* sentence.
sentence

index   An alphabetized list of special names and topics
discussed in a book. The index, usually found in the
back of a book, tells on what page a topic may be
found.

Example:

A
Abilene, 175
Alabama, 17, 46, 89
Alga, 22
Arizona, 43, 187

B
Bill of Rights, 4, 150
Boa, rosy, 189
Boone, Daniel, 100
Boston Tea Party, 199

inference   A conclusion usually based on facts or evidence.

Examples:

What inference did you make when the motor
lost power?

What inference did you make when you saw
lipstick on the rim of the cup?

initial
The first letter of a word or name.

✳ RULES

● Initials used in people's names are capitalized and followed by a period.

Examples:

Thomas Ralph Jones   T. R. Jones

Julie Collins Morley   J. C. Morley

● Initials for other proper nouns are capitalized and often followed by a period.

Examples: U.S.A.   P.O.

Exceptions: NASA   PTA

integer
Any whole number. Negative numbers, positive numbers, and zero are integers.

Examples: $-319, -42, 0, 1, 3, 257$

interrogative sentence
See sentence.

irregular verb
See verb, irregular.

key (map) A list of symbols and what they represent; used on a map to show where places can be found. A key is sometimes called a legend.

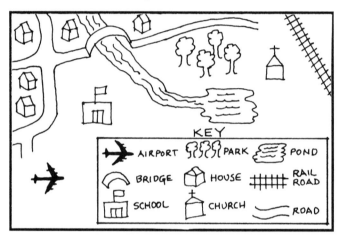

key words Important words that give meaning to sentences. Key words help you understand the meaning of a sentence more easily.

Example:

The long *file* of *soldiers* moved slowly.

Key words also help you decide what topic to look for in an index to find more information.

Example:

How do *Eskimos* live in *Alaska?*

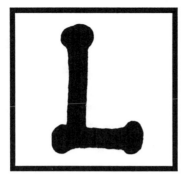

latitude

The distance north or south of the equator measured in degrees. A degree of latitude is about 69 miles. Five lines of latitude are named: the Equator, the Tropic of Cancer, the Tropic of Capricorn, the Arctic Circle, and the Antarctic Circle.

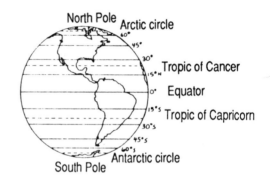

Also see **equator.**

leap year

See **calendar.**

**least
common
denominator
(LCD)**

The smallest multiple of the denominators of two or more fractions. When adding or subtracting fractions, the denominators must be the same number. If not, it is necessary to find the least common denominator before completing the problem.

Example:

$$\frac{2}{3} + \frac{1}{4}$$

The denominators are not the same.

MORE
→

73

FINDING THE LCD

1. Compare the denominators in the fractions to see if one of them can be used as the LCD.
2. If not, list the multiples of the two denominators to find the smallest common multiple which will be the LCD.

$$\frac{2}{3} \qquad 3, \quad 6, \quad 9, \quad 12, \quad 15$$

$$+\frac{1}{4} \qquad 4, \quad 8, \quad 12, \quad 16, \quad 20$$

The LCD is 12.

3. Using the LCD, write the equivalent fraction for each fraction. Remember to divide the LCD by the denominator and then multiply that number by the numerator.

$$\frac{2}{3} \qquad \overline{}\ 12 \qquad 12 \div 3 \times 2 = \frac{8}{12}$$

$$+\frac{1}{4} \qquad \overline{}\ 12 \qquad 12 \div 4 \times 1 = \frac{3}{12}$$

$$\frac{11}{12}$$

✳ **Follow the same steps when subtracting fractions.**

Also see **multiple.**

legend (map)   *See* **key (map).**

less than [<]

A term and symbol used in comparing two numbers. The point of the symbol points to the smaller number.

Examples:

3 < 7   The number 3 is less than 7.

84 < 96   The number 84 is less than 96.

letter writing (business)

There are six main parts in a business letter:

Heading The heading tells the writer's address and the date. Write the heading in the upper right-hand corner of the letter. The first line tells the house address. The second line tells the city, state, and zip code. The third line tells the complete date.

Business Address Begin on the left side of the paper two lines below the heading. Include the name of the person to whom you are writing, the name of the company or place of business, and the address.

Greeting This is the way to say "hello." Write the greeting two lines below the business address. The greeting begins with a capital and is followed by a colon. Unless you know the person well, use her or his last name.

Body This is the news or business part of the letter. Indent the first word in each paragraph.

Closing Write the closing two lines below the body and to the right, lined up with the heading above. Begin the closing with a capital letter and follow with a comma.

Signature Write your full name, unless you know the person well.

---

123 Oak Street
Chicago, Illinois 60610
April 2, 1989

Ms. Mary Carter
A. B. C. Block Company
465 North Wood Road
Ames, Iowa 60456

Dear Ms. Carter:

I received your shipment of blocks today. I am pleased to tell you that I am very satisfied with the product, and with your prompt, courteous service. The blocks are colorful, well made, and appealing and safe for use by children. They will be a welcome addition to our preschool's inventory of toys and playthings.

The children thank you also, and we look forward to doing business with your company in the future. We will recommend your products to the other schools in the area. Please send us a catalog of your other products at your earliest convenience.

Sincerely, *Sally Thompson*
Sally Thompson,
Fun 'n Games Nursery School

MORE →

Sally Thompson
Fun 'n Games Nursery School
123 Oak Street
Chicago, Illinois 60610

Ms. Mary Carter
A. B. C. Block Company
466 North Wood Road
Ames, Iowa 60456

Addressing an Envelope
The form for addressing an envelope is the same for a business or friendly letter. An address may be typed or handwritten.

letter writing (friendly) There are five main parts in a friendly letter:

Heading Follow the same heading as in a business letter.

123 Oak St.
Chicago, Il 60610
December 28, 1990
Dear Mary,
Thank you for the lovely present. It was thoughtful of you to remember my birthday. Please call me next time you're in the area; perhaps we can have lunch.
Thanks again,
Sincerely,
Sally

Greeting This is the way you say "hello." Begin on the left side of the paper three lines below the heading and use a comma after your friend's name. Be sure to use your friend's first name if you know her or him well.

Body Indent the first word in each paragraph. This is the news part of the letter.

Closing This is the way you say "good-bye." Write the closing one line below the body and to the right, lined up with the heading above. The closing always begins with a capital letter and ends with a comma.

Signature Write your name below the closing. Use only your first name if you know your friend well. If not, use your last name, too. Always begin your signature with a capital letter.

longitude
The distance east or west of the Prime Meridian at Greenwich, England; measured in degrees. The Prime Meridian is 0 degrees. The lines of longitude run from the North Pole to the South Pole.

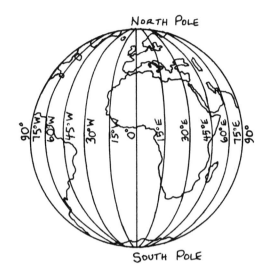

Also see **meridian.**

main topic and subtopics

The main topic of an essay is the subject or main idea. Subtopics tell the details or facts about the main topic.

Also see **outline** and **paragraph.**

math symbols

Marks that represent a math process or element.

+	add
−	subtract
×	multiply
÷	divide
⌐	divide
.	decimal point
=	is equal to
≠	is not equal to
<	is less than
>	is more than, is greater than
[ ]	empty set
Ø	empty set, null set
∪	union of sets
∩	intersection of sets
≈	equivalent
≉	unequivalent
°C	degree Celsius
°F	degree Fahrenheit
+ 6	positive integer
− 6	negative integer
2^4	2 is the base, 4 is the exponent (2x2x2x2)
√	square root
π	pi (3.14159)

mean   *See* average.

measurement   A method of telling size or dimension.

MEASUREMENT CHART

U.S. Customary	Metric
Length and Distance	**Length and Distance**
12 inches (in.) = 1 foot (ft.)	0.1 meter (m) = 1 decimeter (dm)
3 feet = 1 yard (yd.)	0.01 meter = 1 centimeter (cm)
36 inches = 1 yard (yd.)	0.001 meter = 1 millimeter (mm)
1,760 yards = 1 mile (mi.)	10 meters = 1 decameter (dkm)
5,280 feet = 1 mile (mi.)	100 meters = 1 hectometer (hm)
	1,000 meters = 1 kilometer (km)
Liquid Measure	
8 fluid ounces (fl. oz.) = 1 cup (c.)	
16 fluid ounces = 1 pint (pt.)	**Liquid Measure**
2 cups = 1 pint (pt.)	1,000 milliliters (ml) = 1 liter (l)
2 pints = 1 quart (qt.)	10 liters = 1 decaliter (dk)
32 fluid ounces = 1 quart (qt.)	100 liters = 1 hectoliter (h)
4 quarts = 1 gallon (gal.)	1,000 liters = 1 kiloliter (k)
Weight	**Weight**
16 ounces (oz.) = 1 pound (lb.)	10 grams (g) = 1 decagram (dkg)
2,000 pounds = 1 ton (tn.)	100 grams = 1 hectogram (hg)
100 pounds = 1 hundredweight	1,000 grams = 1 kilogram (kg)
(cwt.)	1,000 milligrams (mg) = 1 gram (g)
	1,000 kilograms = 1 metric ton (t)
Dry Measure	
2 pints = 1 quart (qt.)	
8 quarts = 1 peck (pk.)	
4 pecks = 1 bushel (bu.)	

Also see **centimeter.**

meridian

An imaginary circle around the earth passing through the North Pole and the South Pole. The Prime Meridian is the meridian that passes through Greenwich, England, and is 0°. All other meridians or lines of longitude are measured east or west of the Prime Meridian.

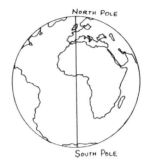

Also see **longitude.**

metaphor

An expression or figure of speech that names or compares one thing to another thing and finds a likeness between them. The words *as*, *like*, or *than* are **not** used in metaphors.

Examples:

Jerry was a *tornado* once he began his work.
"Their laughter *exploded* in the hall," said Gardner.

Also see **simile.**

minuend

A number from which another number (the subtrahend) is being subtracted.

Example:

$$\begin{array}{r} 9 \\ -5 \\ \hline \end{array}$$ The number 9 is the minuend.

Also see **subtraction** and **subtrahend.**

mixed number

A number made up of a whole number and a fraction.

Examples:

$$6\frac{7}{8} \qquad 14\frac{2}{5}$$

money

Coins and paper bills used to pay for goods and services.

Example: U.S. One Dollar = 100 pennies
= 10 dimes
= 20 nickels
= 4 quarters
= 2 half-dollars

SYMBOLS
$ = dollar
¢ = cent

✱ When writing dollars and cents together, it's not necessary to use both symbols.

Examples:

$7.25   25¢

months of the year

See **calendar.**

multiple

A product of a whole number and any other whole number. A number into which another number may be divided with a zero remainder.

Examples:

$3 \times 4 = 12$

The number 12 is a multiple of 3 and 4.

$15 \div 5 = 3$ (0 remainder)

The number 15 is a multiple of 5 and 3.

Some multiples of 4:

Also see **least common denominator (LCD).**

multiplicand The number to be multiplied by another.

> **Example:**
>
> 6 The number 6 is the multiplicand.
> × 8

multiplication A short way of adding a number to itself.

> **Example:**
>
> | **Addition** | or | **Multiplication** |
> |:---:|:---:|:---:|
> | 23 | | 23 |
> | 23 | | × 3 |
> | +23 | | 69 |
> | 69 | | |

MULTIPLYING TWO-PLACE NUMBERS

> **Example:**
>
> 54
> × 36

1. Cover the 3 in the tens place with your finger and multiply the remaining numbers in the usual way.

2. The result (324) is the partial product.

> 54
> × 36
> 324 partial product

3. Cover the 6 in the ones place with your finger. Note that the 3 is in the tens place. When you multiply with the 3, start your answer (partial product) in the tens place.

$$
\begin{array}{r}
54 \\
\times\,36 \\
\hline
324 \\
1620 \\
\hline
\end{array}
\;\text{partial product}
$$

✳ **It helps to put a zero in the ones place, so you won't write in the wrong place.**

4. Add both partial products to get the answer or final product.

$$
\begin{array}{r}
54 \\
\times\,36 \\
\hline
324 \\
1620 \\
\hline
1944 \\
\end{array}
\;\text{final product}
$$

5. Continue these same steps when multiplying 3 place numbers or more. Remember to keep adding zeros so you won't write in the wrong place.

Also see **casting out nines** and **multiplication table.**

multiplication table A chart to help you find the product of two numbers. Use the multiplication table on the next page to find products quickly.

- To multiply two numbers, locate one of your numbers in the left column and the other number in the top row.

- From the left column, trace across, and from the top row, trace down until your fingers meet on a square.

- The number in that square will be your answer or product.

Example:

$4 \times 6 =$

- Find 4 in the left column.

- Find 6 in the top row.

- Using your left hand, move your finger from the 4 across the row as you move a finger on your right hand down the column from the 6. When your fingers meet on a square, you will find that:

$4 \times 6 = 24$

multiplier The number that tells how many times the multiplicand is multiplied.

Example:

$$\begin{array}{r} 4 \\ \times\,9 \\ \hline \end{array}$$ The number 9 is the multiplier.

MULTIPLICATION TABLE

×	1	2	3	4	5	6	7	8	9	10	11	12
1	1	2	3	4	5	6	7	8	9	10	11	12
2	2	4	6	8	10	12	14	16	18	20	22	24
3	3	6	9	12	15	18	21	24	27	30	33	36
4	4	8	12	16	20	24	28	32	36	40	44	48
5	5	10	15	20	25	30	35	40	45	50	55	60
6	6	12	18	24	30	36	42	48	54	60	66	72
7	7	14	21	28	35	42	49	56	63	70	77	84
8	8	16	24	32	40	48	56	64	72	80	88	96
9	9	18	27	36	45	54	63	72	81	90	99	108
10	10	20	30	40	50	60	70	80	90	100	110	120
11	11	22	33	44	55	66	77	88	99	110	121	132
12	12	24	36	48	60	72	84	96	108	120	132	144

negative number

A number that is less than zero, written with a minus sign before the numeral.

$$\xleftarrow{\quad} \overset{-10\ -9\ -8\ -7\ -6\ -5\ -4\ -3\ -2\ -1}{\underset{}{\Big|}} \overset{0}{\Big|} \overset{1\ \ 2\ \ 3\ \ 4\ \ 5\ \ 6\ \ 7\ \ 8\ \ 9\ \ 10}{\underset{}{}} \xrightarrow{\quad}$$

Example:
Ten degrees below zero is written −10°.

nonfiction

A writing about real people and events.

Examples:
A Study of History by Arnold Toynbee
The Sea Around Us by Rachael Carson

noun

A word that names a person, place, or thing.

SOME COMMON NOUNS

Person	Place	Thing
teacher	school	book
boy	home	jet
astronaut	farm	fork
lady	theater	dictionary

PROPER NOUNS

A proper noun names a special person, place, or thing. Always begin a proper noun with a capital letter.

Examples:

Person	Place	Thing
Mrs. Palmer	Chicago	Nintendo
Mayor Jones	Brookfield Zoo	Izod
Coach Miller	Lincoln Memorial	Swatch

POSSESSIVE NOUNS

To make nouns possessive, *see* **apostrophe.**

number line   A line showing numbers in order and at even intervals from the smallest at the left to the greatest at the right.

$$\longleftarrow \; 0 \; 1 \; 2 \; 3 \; 4 \; 5 \; 6 \; 7 \; 8 \; 9 \; 10 \; 11 \; 12 \; 13 \; 14 \; 15 \; 16 \; 17 \; 18 \; 19 \; 20 \; \longrightarrow$$

numeral   A symbol written to represent a number.

Examples: 7, 143, 25

numerator   The number written above the line in a fraction. The numerator tells how many equal parts of a whole is named.

Examples:

$\dfrac{2}{3}$ The number 2 is the numerator.

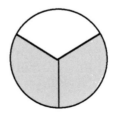

Two parts of three are shaded.

$\dfrac{2}{3}$ of the whole is shaded

Also see **denominator** and **fraction.**

87

oblong   A rectangular or elliptical shape, longer than wide.
                   Examples:

obtuse angle   *See* angle.

ocean   A large body of salt water. There are four great oceans
                   covering about 72 percent of the earth's surface.

Great Oceans	Approx. Area
Pacific	63,800,000 sq. mi.
Atlantic	31,800,000 sq. mi.
Indian	28,400,000 sq. mi.
Arctic	5,400,000 sq. mi.

                   Also see **map of continents** and **world map**.

opinion   *See* **fact or opinion**.

ordinal number

A number stating a position or place. Ordinal numbers can be written in two ways.

Examples:

1st .... first
2nd .... second
3rd .... third
4th .... fourth
5th .... fifth
6th .... sixth
7th .... seventh
8th .... eighth
9th .... ninth
10th .... tenth

Also see **cardinal number.**

outline

A plan of organization that shows the *ideas* of a written work, talk, or project. An outline usually answers the questions: what, how, when, where, and which one.

Form	Sample Outline
Title	Vacations
I. Main Topic	I. Summer
A. Subtopic	A. Camping
B. Subtopic	B. Fishing
C. Subtopic	C. Sightseeing
II. Main Topic	II. Winter
A. Subtopic	A. Skiing
B. Subtopic	B. Tobogganing
C. Subtopic	C. Sightseeing

MORE
→

✳ RULES

● The first word in each main topic and each sub-topic begins with a capital letter.

● Each subtopic is indented under the main topic.

● Use Roman numerals for the main topics and capital letters for the subtopics.

USING AN OUTLINE
IN WRITING AN ESSAY

1. Begin a new paragraph for each main topic and subtopic.
2. Each paragraph must have a topic sentence that tells what that paragraph is about. The topic sentence is usually the first sentence in the paragraph.

Also see **main topic and subtopics.**

P

palindrome

A word that is spelled the same forward or backward.

Examples: | dad | level |
|---|---|
| noon | peep |
| gag | madam |

paragraph

A group of sentences, usually 3 to 5 sentences, that tells about one subject or idea. This thought or idea is called the *main idea* of the *paragraph*. The main idea is usually stated in the first sentence called a *topic sentence*. The first word of a paragraph is usually indented.

✳ HELP

● Good paragraphs include:
One main idea
One topic sentence
Three to five detail sentences

Example:

When you adopt a dog or a cat, you will be responsible for taking good care of your pet. You must provide good food, a balanced diet, plenty of fresh water to drink, and a clean and quiet place for sleeping. Your pet will need to visit a doctor to get booster shots to prevent illness. In addition, you must give your pet a nice area for exercise and play, and most important, lots of love.

✳ **The topic sentence is the first sentence.**

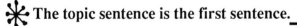

parallel lines   Two or more straight lines that are an equal distance apart at all points.

Example:

---

parentheses
[( )]   Punctuation marks used to enclose a word, phrase, clause, or sentence that is included to give further explanation or comment.

Examples:

I like to go to the theater (the one next to the mall).

(Did you forget the tickets?)

 **RULES**

● If the parentheses occur within a sentence, the punctuation mark goes outside the parentheses.

● If the parentheses contain a complete sentence that stands alone, the punctuation mark goes inside the parentheses.

parts of speech   In grammar, the names of words that function in different ways: nouns, pronouns, verbs, adjectives, adverbs, prepositions, conjunctions, and interjections.

Also see **adjective; adverb; conjunction; noun; preposition; pronoun; verb;** and **verb, irregular.**

past tense   *See* **verb, irregular.**

percent

A hundredth part. Percent tells how many out of 100 are being talked about. The symbol for percent is %.

Example: 80% means 80 of 100

PERCENT TO FRACTION

To change a percent to a common fraction or mixed number, drop the percent sign and write the percent number as a fraction with 100 as the denominator. Reduce to lowest terms.

Examples:

$$25\% \ = \ \frac{25}{100} \ = \ \frac{1}{4}$$

$$155\% = \frac{155}{100} = 1\frac{55}{100} = 1\frac{11}{20}$$

PERCENT TO DECIMAL

To change a percent to a decimal, drop the % sign and multiply by .01. Don't forget to move the decimal point 2 places to the *left*.

Examples:

$$25\% \ = \ 25 \times .01 = .25$$
$$7.3\% \ = \ 7.3 \times .01 = .073$$

DECIMAL TO PERCENT

To change a decimal to a percent, multiply by 100 and add the % sign. The decimal point is moved *2* places to the *right*.

Examples:

$$.52 \ \times 100 = \ 52 \text{ or } 52\%$$
$$.06 \ \times 100 = \ 6 \text{ or } 6\%$$
$$2.5 \ \times 100 = \ 250 \text{ or } 250\%$$

93

FRACTION TO PERCENT

To change a fraction to a percent, divide the numerator by the denominator, multiply the quotient by 100, and add the percent sign.

Example: Change $\dfrac{1}{4}$ to a percent.

$$
\begin{array}{r}
.25 \\
4\overline{)1.00} \\
\underline{8} \\
20 \\
\underline{20} \\
00
\end{array}
$$

.25 × 100 = 25 or 25%

COMMON PERCENT-FRACTION-DECIMAL EQUIVALENTS

Percent	Fraction	Decimal
$12\frac{1}{2}\%$	$\frac{1}{8}$	.125
25%	$\frac{1}{4}$	.25
$33\frac{1}{3}\%$	$\frac{1}{3}$	.333
50%	$\frac{1}{2}$	.50
$62\frac{1}{2}\%$	$\frac{5}{8}$	.625
$66\frac{2}{3}\%$	$\frac{2}{3}$	.666
75%	$\frac{3}{4}$	.75
$87\frac{1}{2}\%$	$\frac{7}{8}$	.875

Also see **decimal, equivalent,** and **fraction.**

perimeter

The distance around the sides of a figure such as a square or rectangle. To find the perimeter, measure the lengths of the sides and add.

Example:

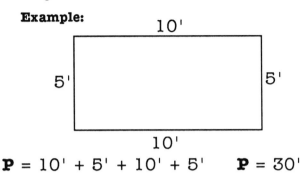

$$P = 10' + 5' + 10' + 5' \qquad P = 30'$$

period [.]

A punctuation mark used to mark the end of a sentence or to show an abbreviation.

Examples:
Lisa bought a new dress.
Dr. and Mrs. Wilson

Also see **abbreviation.**

perpendicular lines

Two intersecting lines that form right angles.

Also see **angle.**

phrase

A group of words that has meaning but is not a complete sentence. A phrase does not contain a subject and a predicate.

Examples: in the park
at the beach

Also see **preposition** and **prepositional phrase.**

pi [π]

A letter in the Greek alphabet; a letter that represents approximately 3.14159, the ratio of a circumference of a curve to its diameter.

Also see **circumference.**

planet

A heavenly body in the solar system; a planet moves around the sun. There are nine planets in the solar system:

Mercury	Saturn
Venus	Uranus
Earth	Neptune
Mars	Pluto
Jupiter	

An easy way to remember the planets in the order of their distance from the sun:

My Very Easy Method—Just Set Up Nine Planets.

plural

The form of a word that means more than one.

✳ RULES

● To form the plural of most nouns, add *s.*

Examples:

girl	girl*s*
truck	truck*s*
pin	pin*s*
shoe	shoe*s*
flower	flower*s*
steps	step*s*

● Add *es* to singular nouns that end in the following letters:

s	ss	sh	ch	x	z

Examples:

gas	gas*es*
mass	mass*es*
bush	bush*es*
church	church*es*
fox	fox*es*
buzz	buzz*es*

● Add *es* to some words that end in *o*.

Examples:

potato	potato*es*
hero	hero*es*

Some exceptions:

radio	radio*s*
piano	piano*s*

● When singular nouns end in a consonant and *y*, change the *y* to *i* and add *es*.

Examples:

story	stor*ies*
baby	bab*ies*
lady	lad*ies*

● For most nouns ending in *f* or *fe*, change the *f* to *v* and add *es*.

Examples:

knife	kni*ves*
loaf	loa*ves*
thief	thie*ves*
half	hal*ves*

● Some nouns have the same spelling for singular and plural forms.

Examples:

deer	deer
sheep	sheep
moose	moose
trout	trout

97

● Some nouns form plurals by changing their spelling.

Examples:

man	men
child	children
goose	geese
foot	feet
mouse	mice
woman	women

Also see **apostrophe** and **verbs.**

p.m.

Post meridiem; used to show the time from after noon to midnight.

Examples:

3:00 p.m.   8:30 p.m.   11:59 p.m.

possessive nouns

See **apostrophe.**

predicate

Word or words in a sentence that tell something about the subject. The predicate includes a verb and often includes objects or words that modify or complement the verb or a noun.

Examples:

Phillip *lost his tennis racket.*
Pat *is talking on the phone.*
Mom *gave me a cookie.*
Her sister *is a doctor.*

prefix

A syllable added to the beginning of a word to change the meaning of the word.

SOME COMMON PREFIXES

Prefix	Meaning	Example
auto-	self	automatic, autograph
bi-	two	bicycle, bilingual
com-	with, together	compound, commit
con-	with	connect, conform
de-	down, from	deflate, depart
dis-	not	dishonest, disappear
ex-	out	export, exclude
mis-	wrong	misspell, misplace
non-	not	nonliving, nonskid
pre-	before	preschool, prepaid
re-	again, back	reheat, return
trans-	across	transform, transport
tri-	three	tricycle, triplets
un-	not, opposite of	unhappy, unclean
uni-	one	unicycle, unicorn

preposition

A word that relates a noun or pronoun to some other word in a sentence. A preposition is followed by an object and begins a prepositional phrase.

Example:
He put the present *on the table.*

SOME COMMON PREPOSITIONS

about	around	by	in	on	toward
above	at	down	into	out	under
across	before	during	near	over	until
after	behind	for	of	through	with
along	below	from	off	to	without

prepositional phrase

A phrase beginning with a preposition and ending with a noun or pronoun. The phrase modifies a noun, pronoun, verb, or adjective and shows a relationship in time or space.

Example:

In a few minutes, the man *on the boat* will dive *into the water.*

present tense

See **verb.**

presidents of the United States

See chart of **Presidents of the United States** on opposite page.

primary colors

In art, the colors red, yellow, and blue. Combinations of these primary colors may be mixed to produce all other colors.

product

The result of multiplying one number by another number; the answer to a multiplication problem.

Examples:

$$\begin{array}{r} 6 \\ \times\,2 \\ \hline 12 \end{array}$$ The number 12 is the product.

$$75 \times 22 = 1,650$$

The number 1,650 is the product.

Also see **casting out nines** and **multiplication.**

PRESIDENTS OF THE UNITED STATES

Name	Term
1st............George Washington.............1789-1797
2nd..........John Adams.........................1797-1801
3rd...........Thomas Jefferson.................1801-1809
4th...........James Madison.....................1809-1817
5th............James Monroe......................1817-1825
6th...........John Quincy Adams.............1825-1829
7th...........Andrew Jackson..................1829-1837
8th...........Martin Van Buren...............1837-1841
9th...........William H. Harrison...........1841
10th.........John Tyler...........................1841-1845
11th.........James K. Polk.....................1845-1849
12th.........Zachary Taylor....................1849-1850
13th.........Millard Fillmore..................1850-1853
14th.........Franklin Pierce....................1853-1857
15th.........James Buchanan...................1857-1861
16th.........Abraham Lincoln.................1861-1865
17th.........Andrew Johnson.................1865-1869
18th.........Ulysses S. Grant..................1869-1877
19th.........Rutherford B. Hayes...........1877-1881
20th.........James A. Garfield...............1881
21st..........Chester A. Arthur...............1881-1885
22nd........Grover Cleveland................1885-1889
23rd.........Benjamin Harrison.............1889-1893
24th.........Grover Cleveland...............1893-1897
25th.........William McKinley.............1897-1901
26th.........Theodore Roosevelt...........1901-1909
27th.........William H. Taft..................1909-1913
28th.........Woodrow Wilson...............1913-1921
29th.........Warren G. Harding............1921-1923
30th.........Calvin Coolidge.................1923-1929
31st..........Herbert Hoover...................1929-1933
32nd........Franklin D. Roosevelt.........1933-1945
33rd.........Harry S. Truman.................1945-1953
34th.........Dwight D. Eisenhower........1953-1961
35th.........John F. Kennedy.................1961-1963
36th.........Lyndon B. Johnson.............1963-1969
37th.........Richard M. Nixon..............1969-1974
38th.........Gerald R. Ford...................1974-1977
39th.........James E. Carter, Jr. 1977-1981
40th.........Ronald W. Reagan.............1981-1989
41st..........George H. W. Bush............1989-

pronoun A word used in place of a noun. A word that refers to a noun.

SINGULAR PRONOUNS

I, me, my, mine, myself
you, your, yours, yourself
he, him, his, himself
she, her, hers, herself
it, its, itself

PLURAL PRONOUNS

we, us, our, ours, ourselves
you, your, yours, yourselves
they, them, their, theirs, themselves

pronunciation key A list of symbols that shows how letters in words are pronounced.

SAMPLE PRONUNCIATION KEY

ă	fat	ŏ	lot	ŭ	cut	ə	alone
ā	say	ō	go	ûr	fur	ə	item
âr	share	ô	for	ûr	term	ə	pencil
ä	father	ô	taught	ûr	firm	ə	atom
ĕ	let	ô	saw	ûr	word	ə	circus
ē	be	oi	foil	ûr	heard	zh	garage
ĭ	pit	o͝o	book	th	bath	zh	measure
ī	fight	o͞o	boot	th	bathe	zh	vision
îr	pierce	ou	out				

proofreading symbols Symbols used by an editor or proofreader to let the writer or printer know what changes or corrections are to be made in written or printed material.

Symbol	Meaning	Mark on Paper	Corrected
⌗	begin a new paragraph	He ran fast. ⌗The race ended.	He ran fast. The race ended.
⋀	insert a letter or word	The ⌄ʳace	The race
⋀	insert a comma	A bright⌄cheerful young boy	A bright, cheerful young boy
⊙	insert a period	She sat down⋀	She sat down.
ℯ	take out	Anns went home.	Ann went home.
cap	make a capital	The white house	The White House
lc	make a lower case	at the Park	at the park
⋎	insert an apostrophe	Tims bat	Tim's bat
⌄⌄	quotation marks needed	⌄Get ready.⌄	"Get ready."
⌒	close up space	An ani mal	An animal

103

Example:

UNEDITED

i plege allegiaence to the flage the United

states of america and to the republic for

whitch it stands one nation Under God,

indivisile with liberty and gustice for all

EDITED

i plege allegiaence to the flage the United

states of america and to the republic for

whitch it stands one nation Under God,

indivisile with liberty and gustice for all

FINAL

I pledge allegiance to the flag of the United

States of America and to the republic for

which it stands, one nation under God, indi-

visible, with liberty and justice for all.

proverb   A short, wise saying that tells a truth.

Examples:
Better safe than sorry.
One good turn deserves another.
A stitch in time saves nine.
He who hesitates is lost.
The only way to have a friend is to be one.

Q

quotation   The exact words said or written by someone else.

Example:
"Ask not what your country can do for you; ask what you can do for your country."

John Fitzgerald Kennedy

quotation marks [" "]   A pair of punctuation marks used to show spoken or written conversation, words, and titles.

✳ RULES

● **Direct Quotation** Place quotation marks at the beginning and end of the exact word or words said or written by someone.

Examples:
Judy said, "My work is almost finished."
"Why can't I go?" asked Don.

● **Divided Quotation** When a quotation is divided, place quotation marks only around exact words spoken.

Examples:
"My favorite ice cream flavor," said Tim, "is strawberry."
"I'm hungry," said Jim. "What's for dinner?"

MORE
→

105

● **New Speaker** Use quotation marks in written conversation and start a new paragraph every time the speaker changes.

Examples:

"What's your favorite food?" asked Betsy while they were waiting for the bus.

"Pizza," replied Charlie, with a hungry look in his eye.

"Oh, I like to eat hot dogs," answered Betsy.

"I love all foods," sighed Charlie.

● **Special Words** Use quotation marks with words used to show a special sense.

Examples:

The "expert" made three mistakes.

The engine started with a "bang."

● **Short Works** Use quotation marks with titles of short works like stories, poems, television programs, reports, short plays, or musical compositions.

Examples:

"Sesame Street" is my brother's favorite program.

My report is called "Apes."

● **Quote within a Quote** Use single quotation marks when you quote within a quotation.

Example:

The parent explained to the teacher, "My child told me, 'I don't have to do a report,' but is that true?"

quotient

The answer to a division problem.

Examples:

$$2 \overline{\smash{\big)}\, 16}^{\ 8}$$

The number 8 is the quotient.

$24 \div 6 = 4$ The number 4 is the quotient.

Also see **casting out nines** and **division.**

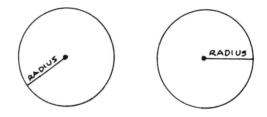

radius

The shortest distance from the center of a circle to any point on the circle.

ratio

The relationship or comparison in size, amount, or number between two things.

Example:

10 children and 1 scout leader
The ratio is 10 to 1 or 10:1.

remainder

The number left when one number cannot be divided evenly by another number.

Example:

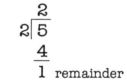

Also see **casting out nines** and **division.**

renaming   Naming numbers with a different set of numbers; regrouping numbers; used to regroup numbers to the next place value.

HELP

1. Add the digits in the ones place first.

```
          ones
  467      7
+287     +7
         14
```

2. Write the 4 in the ones column and give the 1 ten to the tens column. Add the digits in the tens column.

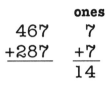

```
   ①        tens
  467       ⓪6
+287       +8
    4       15
```

3. Write the 5 in the tens column and give the 1 hundred (10 tens) to the hundreds column. Add the column.

```
  ① ①     hundreds
  467       ⓪4
+287       +2
   54        7
```

4. Write the 7 in the hundreds column.

```
  467
+287
 754
```

Also see **borrowing** and **casting out nines**.

right angle   *See* angle.

Roman numerals   A number system used by the Romans in which 7 basic letters were given specific values.

$$I = 1$$
$$V = 5$$
$$X = 10$$
$$L = 50$$
$$C = 100$$
$$D = 500$$
$$M = 1,000$$

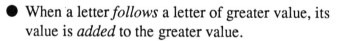

● When a letter is repeated, its value is repeated.

$$I = 1$$
$$II = 2$$
$$X = 10$$
$$XX = 20$$
$$C = 100$$
$$CCC = 300$$

● When a letter *follows* a letter of greater value, its value is *added* to the greater value.

$$XV = 15 \ (10 + 5)$$
$$LX = 60 \ (50 + 10)$$

● When a letter of smaller value is *before* a letter of greater value, its value is *subtracted* from the greater value.

$$IV = 4 \ (1 \text{ from } 5)$$
$$XL = 40 \ (10 \text{ from } 50)$$
$$CD = 400 \ (100 \text{ from } 500)$$

root word   *See* base word.

rounding   Writing a whole number to the nearest ten, hundred, thousand, or greater place value. Use rounding when you don't need an exact number.

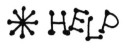

- For numbers 1, 2, 3, 4, round down to the lower 10, 100, 1,000, etc.

Example: Round 43 to the nearest 10.

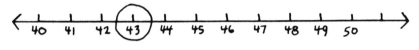

43 rounded is 40

- For numbers 5, 6, 7, 8, 9, round up to the higher 10, 100, 1,000, etc.

Example: Round 572 to the nearest 100.

572 rounded is 600

Example: Round 1500 to the nearest 1000.

1500 rounded is 2000

S

schwa [ə]

An unstressed or unaccented vowel sound in a syllable. The (ə) can represent any vowel.

> **Examples:** about .... ə -bout'
> item .... i' təm
> April .... A' prəl
> parrot ..... par' ət
> circus ...... cir' cəs

semicolon [;]

A punctuation mark that shows a separation in a sentence not as complete as a period, but more complete than a comma.

✷ RULES

● Use a semicolon between two separate thoughts in a sentence not connected by *and, but, or, so, for, yet,* or *nor.*

Example:
I have an idea; Jerry has a good idea, too.

● Use a semicolon between a list of things if the things contain commas.

Example:
The class officers are Carol Brown, President; Terry Smith, Vice-President; Bob Robb, Secretary; and Roy Toy, Treasurer.

112

● Use a semicolon before a conjunctive adverb (an adverb that connects) when it separates two strong statements.

Example:

Climbing this mountain is difficult; however, it is very exciting.

sentence A group of words that tells a complete idea or thought. Sentences have a subject and a predicate.

 ✳ KINDS OF SENTENCES

● **Declarative** (Statement) A sentence that tells or states an idea and ends with a period.

Example: We will go to the zoo.

● **Interrogative** (Question) A sentence that asks something and ends with a question mark.

Example: What time is the game?

● **Imperative** (Command or Request) A sentence that tells you to do something; the imperative sentence can end with either a period or an exclamation mark.

Examples: Don't touch the oven!
Please pass the paper.

● **Exclamatory** (Exclamation) A sentence that shows excitement or surprise and ends with an exclamation mark.

Examples: I found five dollars!
What an exciting show!

sequence The order or following of one thing after another. Sequencing in stories tells what happens first, next, and last.

> **Example:**
> ### Incorrect Sequence
> She ate breakfast.
> Paula woke up early.
> She rode her bike to school.
>
> ### Correct Sequence
> Paula woke up early.
> She ate breakfast.
> She rode her bike to school.

silent letter A vowel or consonant that is not sounded in a word.

> **Examples:**
> knot ....The *k* is not sounded.
> gnaw ....The *g* is not sounded.
> czar................The *c* is not sounded.
> wrong.............The *w* is not sounded.
> psychic ....The *p* is not sounded.

simile A comparison in which two unlike things are compared; the words *as, like,* or *than* are used.

> **Examples:**
> Bob was as red *as* a lobster.
> Jim is *like* a starved animal.
> Katie has grown taller *than* a giraffe.

singular The form of a word that means one of something.

> **Examples:**   book   eye
>   cola   girl
>   crayon   turkey

Use the word *a, an,* or *the* in front of a singular noun.

Examples: a toy
an alligator
the cart

Also see **apostrophe, pronoun,** and **verb.**

**spelling
rules**

For every spelling rule in the English language, there is usually at least one exception.

For all words:
1. Look at the word. Say the word.
2. Listen to the sounds the letters make.
3. Picture the word in your mind.
4. Memorize the tricky parts of the word.
5. Say the word again and write it.

● When adding prefixes to a word, the spelling of the base word stays the same.

Examples: un lucky   *unlucky*
re wind   *rewind*

● When adding the suffix *-ly* to words ending in *l,* keep the final *l* and add *ly.*

Examples: real *ly*   real*ly*
beautiful *ly*   beautiful*ly*

● When adding the suffix *-ness* to words ending in *n,* keep the final *n* and add *ness.*

Examples: sudden *ness*   sudden*ness*
mean *ness*   mean*ness*

● When adding a suffix beginning with a vowel to a base word ending in silent *e,* drop the silent *e* and add the suffix.

Examples: have *ing*   hav*ing*

             nice *est*   nic*est*

             please *ed*   plea*sed*

● When adding a suffix beginning with a consonant to a base word ending in a silent *e,* keep the final *e.*

Examples: nine *ty*   nine*ty*

             grace *ful*   grace*ful*

             amuse *ment* amuse*ment*

Exceptions: argue *ment*   argu*ment*

              judge *ment*   judg*ment*

              nine *th*   nin*th*

              true *ly*   tru*ly*

● When adding a suffix to a base word that ends in *y* with a consonant before it, change the *y* to *i* and add the suffix.

Examples: happy *ness* happ*iness*

             greedy *est* greed*iest*

             hurry *ed*   hurr*ied*

Exceptions: cry *ing*   cry*ing*

              bury *ing*   bury*ing*

              try *ing*   try*ing*

              copy *ing*   copy*ing*

● When adding a suffix to a base word that ends in *y* with a vowel before it, keep the *y.*

Examples: relay *ing* relay*ing*

             play *ing*   play*ing*

Exceptions: pay *ed* pa*id*

              say *ed* sa*id*

              day *ly* da*ily*

● In words of one syllable with one vowel followed by one consonant, double the final consonant when adding a suffix.

Examples: run *ing* run*ning*

thin *er* thin*ner*

stop *ed* stop*ped*

● When adding a suffix that begins with a vowel to a word of two or more syllables that ends with a consonant, double the final consonant when the word ends with a consonant-vowel-consonant and the accent is on the last syllable.

Examples: be gin *ing* begin*ning*

re fer *ing* refer*ring*

o mit *ing* omit*ting*

● If a word ends in *x, z, ch, sh,* or *ss*, add *es* to form the plural.

Examples: box *es*   box*es*

buzz *es*   buzz*es*

church *es*   church*es*

lash *es*   lash*es*

dress *es*   dress*es*

● Memorizing this rhyme will help you remember the *ie* and *ei* rule.

I before *e*

Except after *c,*

Or when sounded as *a*

As in n*ei*ghbor or w*ei*gh.

Examples: s*ie*ve

rec*ei*ve

Exceptions: cons*cie*nce

so*cie*ty

117

states   *See* United States of America.

straight   *See* angle.
angle

stress mark   A mark used with words of more than one syllable to
[′]   show which syllable is said more strongly.

> **Examples:** accent (ac′ cent)
>   repeat (re - peat′)

PRIMARY STRESS OR ACCENT MARK (′)

Another name for stress mark is primary accent
mark. Shows which syllable is said louder than any
other syllable.

> **Examples:** vanish (van′ish)

SECONDARY STRESS
OR ACCENT MARK (′)

Shows which syllable is said with force but not as
loud as the syllable with the greatest stress.

> **Examples:**   invitation (in′ vi - ta′ tion)
>   multiply (mul′ ti - ply′)

subject   A word or group of words about which something is
          said in a sentence.

> **Examples:**
> *Cindy* is crying.
> *A tall tree* was hit by lightning.
> *The mountains in Alaska* are very high.

Also see **sentence.**

subtopic   *See* **main topic and subtopics** and **outline.**

subtraction   The process of taking away one number from a another number. The remaining amount is called the difference or remainder.

Example:

The number 6 is the difference or remainder.

WORDS THAT TELL YOU
WHEN TO SUBTRACT

How many are left?
Decrease by . . .
How many remain?
Find the difference between . . .
How many fewer . . .
less
take away
minus

PARTS OF A SUBTRACTION PROBLEM

$$\begin{array}{rl} 56 & \text{minuend} \\ -36 & \text{subtrahend} \\ \hline 20 & \text{difference or remainder} \end{array}$$

Also see **borrowing** and **casting out nines.**

subtrahend	The number being subtracted from the minuend in a subtraction problem.

> **Example:**
>
> $$\begin{array}{r} 7 \\ -\underline{5} \end{array}$$	The number 5 is the subtrahend.

Also see **minuend** and **subtraction.**

suffix	A syllable added to the end of a word to make a new word.

SOME COMMON SUFFIXES

Suffix	Meaning	Example
-able	can do	capable
-ance	state of being	resistance
-ed	past tense	annoyed
-er	person who does	teacher
-er	state of being more	warmer
-est	state of being most	biggest
-ful	full of	beautiful
-ish	somewhat like	babyish
-ist	one who does	artist
-ive	tending to	impressive
-less	without	hopeless
-ly	characteristic of	fatherly
-ment	act or state of	amusement
-ness	quality of	darkness
-ship	condition of	hardship
-sion	act or state of	confusion
-tion	act or state of	election
-y	state of	rainy

sum

The answer to an addition problem.

Example:

$$52$$
$$+38$$
$$\overline{90}$$ The number 90 is the sum.

Also see **addition.**

syllable

A part of a word that is pronounced separately. Dividing a word into syllables makes it easier to pronounce.

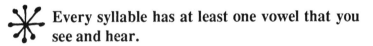 Every syllable has at least one vowel that you see and hear.

Examples:

cat	1 vowel = 1 syllable
per - son	2 vowels = 2 syllables
i - de - a	3 vowels = 3 syllables

Sometimes a syllable has more than one vowel. The second vowel is silent.

Examples: treat

be - tween

✳ RULES

● A one-syllable word cannot be divided.

Examples: dog

mice

● Divide compound words between the two words.

Examples: play-ground

fire-fighter

● Divide words between a prefix and the base word.

Examples: *re*-turn

　　　　　　 mis-place

● Divide words between the base word and a suffix.

Examples: help-*ful*

　　　　　　 cool-*ness*

● If there are two or more consonants between two vowels, divide the word between the first two consonants.

Examples: la*d*-*der*

　　　　　　 chi*l*-*dr*en

● If the first vowel in a word is short and is followed by one consonant, divide the word after the consonant.

Examples: rŏb-in

　　　　　　 măg-ic

● If the first vowel in a word is long and is followed by one consonant, divide the word before the consonant.

Examples: spī-der

　　　　　　 lō-cate

● If a vowel is sounded alone in a word, that vowel forms a syllable by itself.

Examples: dis-a-gree

　　　　　　 u-nit

● If two vowels are together in a word and each makes a separate sound, divide the word between the two vowels.

Examples: *gi*-ant

　　　　　　 i-de-a

● If a word ends with a consonant followed by the letters *le*, divide the word before the consonant.

Examples: ta-*ble*
bi-cy-*cle*

synonym   A word that has the same meaning as another word in the same language.

Examples:

beautiful lovely, pretty, attractive

loud noisy, boisterous, uproarious

Also see **antonym** and **thesaurus.**

T

table of contents

A listing found in the beginning of a book or magazine that tells the chapter titles, topics, or subjects found in the book and the number of the page on which they begin. Sometimes it is written simply as *Contents*.

Example:

Table of Contents

their - there - they're

The word *their* is an adjective that tells *ownership*.

Examples:

They enjoyed *their* trip to Disneyland.

These are *their* books.

The word *there* is an adverb that means *in that place*.

Examples:

Who is *there*?

We will go *there* later.

The word *they're* is a contraction. *They're* means *they are.*

Example:
I am glad *they're* here now.
They're driving to Toledo.

thermometer　An instrument that measures temperature; an instrument with a glass bulb and tube marked with a scale and containing mercury or other liquid which rises or falls as the temperature changes.

Also see **Celsius thermometer** and **Fahrenheit thermometer.**

thesaurus　A book of synonyms or words that have similar meanings. Some thesauruses also include antonyms, or opposites, for each synonym.

Example:
large — big, huge, massive, enormous, immense, grand, gigantic.
Antonym: small, little, tiny, petite.

time　The moment when something occurs. The duration of or how long events and happenings take.

The two hands on a clock or watch tell what time it is.

The *hour hand* is the *shorter* hand. It tells the hour.

The *minute hand* is the *longer* hand. It tells how many minutes before or after the hour.

5:40 or   7:25
20 minutes before 6

TIME

60 seconds (sec.)	1 minute (min.)
60 minutes	1 hour (hr.)
24 hours	1 day (d.)
7 days	1 week (wk.)
4 weeks	1 month (mo.)
52 weeks	1 year (yr.)
12 months	1 year
10 years	1 decade
100 years	1 century (c.)
1000 years	A millennium

Also see **calendar.**

time line   A diagram that gives information about historical happenings, dates, and events at a glance.

Example:

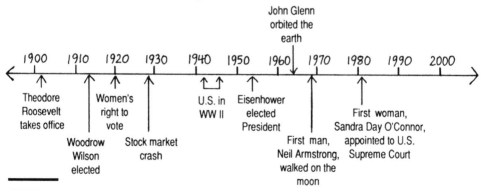

time zones

There are 4 time zones in the continental United States: Pacific, Mountain, Central, and Eastern. Alaska and Hawaii are in separate time zones.

Also see **United States of America map** on page 132.

to - too - two

The word *to* shows the way or gives direction.

Examples:
Please come *to* my party.
We read words from left *to* right.

The word *too* means also or more than enough.

Examples: I am tired, *too.*
I ate *too* much.

The word *two* means a number.

Examples:
Tom has *two* pets: a dog and a cat.
I ate *two* pieces of cake.

topic sentence

The sentence in a paragraph that tells the main idea of a paragraph. The topic sentence is often the first sentence in a paragraph.

Also see **main topic and subtopics** and **paragraph.**

Tropic of Cancer

An imaginary line 1600 miles (23° 27') north of the equator; the northern boundary of the tropical zone. In the tropics, where the sun shines down almost straight at noon every day, the weather is very warm.

Also see **latitude.**

Tropic of Capricorn

An imaginary line 1600 miles (23° 27') south of the equator; the southern boundary of the tropical zone. The sun is almost directly overhead at noon every day, and the temperatures are quite high.

Also see **latitude.**

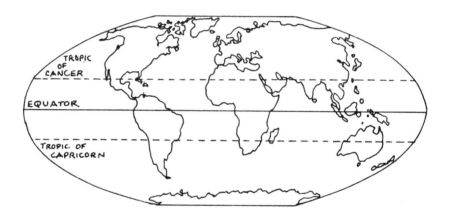

U

United States of America

A republic comprising 50 states and Washington, D.C., the District of Columbia, the nation's capital. Forty-eight states are located in continental U.S.A; Alaska is in North America and Hawaii in the South Pacific. The U.S.A. has coastlines on three oceans: the Atlantic, the Pacific, and the Arctic. In this land of contrasting environments, altitudes range from 282 feet below sea level in Death Valley, California, to 20,320 feet above sea level, the peak of Mt. McKinley in Alaska.

Also see **United States of America list** on pages 130 and 131 and **United States of America map** on page 132.

UNITED STATES OF AMERICA

State	Abbrev.	Capital	State Nickname	State Flower	State Bird	Admitted
Alabama	AL	Montgomery	Heart of Dixie	Camellia	Yellowhammer	1819
Alaska	AK	Juneau	Last Frontier	Forget-Me-Not	Willow Ptarmigan	1959
Arizona	AZ	Phoenix	Grand Canyon State	Saguaro	Cactus Wren	1912
Arkansas	AR	Little Rock	Land of Opportunity	Apple Blossom	Mockingbird	1836
California	CA	Sacramento	Golden State	Golden Poppy	Calif. Valley Quail	1850
Colorado	CO	Denver	Centennial State	Rocky Mt. Columbine	Lark Bunting	1876
Connecticut *	CT	Hartford	Constitution State	Mountain Laurel	Robin	1788
Delaware *	DE	Dover	First State	Peach Blossom	Blue Hen Chicken	1787
Florida	FL	Tallahassee	Sunshine State	Orange Blossom	Mockingbird	1845
Georgia *	GA	Atlanta	Empire State of the South	Cherokee Rose	Brown Thrasher	1788
Hawaii	HI	Honolulu	Aloha State	Hibiscus	Hawaiian Goose	1959
Idaho	ID	Boise	Gem State	Syringa	Mountain Bluebird	1890
Illinois	IL	Springfield	Land of Lincoln	Native Violet	Cardinal	1818
Indiana	IN	Indianapolis	Hoosier State	Peony	Cardinal	1816
Iowa	IA	Des Moines	Hawkeye State	Wild Rose	Eastern Goldfinch	1846
Kansas	KS	Topeka	Sunflower State	Sunflower	Western Meadowlark	1861
Kentucky	KY	Frankfort	Bluegrass State	Goldenrod	Cardinal	1792
Louisiana	LA	Baton Rouge	Pelican State	Magnolia	Brown Pelican	1812
Maine	ME	Augusta	Pine Tree State	White Pine Cone	Chickadee	1820
Maryland*	MD	Annapolis	Old Line State	Black-eyed Susan	Baltimore Oriole	1788
Massachusetts*	MA	Boston	Bay State	Mayflower	Chickadee	1788
Michigan	MI	Lansing	Wolverine State	Apple Blossom	Robin	1837
Minnesota	MN	St. Paul	Gopher State	Lady's Slipper	Loon	1858
Mississippi	MS	Jackson	Magnolia State	Magnolia	Mockingbird	1817
Missouri	MO	Jefferson City	Show Me State	Hawthorn	Bluebird	1821

State	Abbr.	Capital	Nickname	Flower	Bird	Year
Montana	MT	Helena	Treasure State	Bitterroot	Western Meadowlark	1889
Nebraska	NE	Lincoln	Cornhusker State	Goldenrod	Western Meadowlark	1867
Nevada	NV	Carson City	Silver State	Sagebrush	Mountain Bluebird	1864
New Hampshire *	NH	Concord	Granite State	Purple Lilac	Purple Finch	1788
New Jersey *	NJ	Trenton	Garden State	Purple Violet	Eastern Goldfinch	1787
New Mexico	NM	Santa Fe	Land of Enchantment	Yucca	Roadrunner	1912
New York *	NY	Albany	Empire State	Rose	Bluebird	1788
North Carolina *	NC	Raleigh	Tar Heel State	Dogwood	Cardinal	1789
North Dakota	ND	Bismarck	Flickertail State	Wild Prairie Rose	Western Meadowlark	1889
Ohio	OH	Columbus	Buckeye State	Scarlet Carnation	Cardinal	1803
Oklahoma	OK	Oklahoma City	Sooner State	Mistletoe	Scissortail Flycatcher	1907
Oregon	OR	Salem	Beaver State	Oregon Grape	Western Meadowlark	1859
Pennsylvania *	PA	Harrisburg	Keystone State	Mountain Laurel	Ruffed Grouse	1787
Rhode Island *	RI	Providence	Little Rhody	Violet	Rhode Island Red	1790
South Carolina *	SC	Columbia	Palmetto State	Carolina Jessamine	Carolina Wren	1788
South Dakota	SD	Pierre	Coyote State	American Pasqueflower	Ring-necked Pheasant	1889
Tennessee	TN	Nashville	Volunteer State	Iris	Mockingbird	1796
Texas	TX	Austin	Lone Star State	Bluebonnet	Mockingbird	1845
Utah	UT	Salt Lake City	Beehive State	Sego Lily	Sea Gull	1896
Vermont	VT	Montpelier	Green Mountain State	Red Clover	Hermit Thrush	1791
Virginia *	VA	Richmond	Old Dominion	Dogwood	Cardinal	1788
Washington	WA	Olympia	Evergreen State	Coast Rhododendron	Willow Goldfinch	1889
West Virginia	WV	Charleston	Mountain State	Rhododendron	Cardinal	1863
Wisconsin	WI	Madison	Badger State	Wood Violet	Robin	1848
Wyoming	WY	Cheyenne	Equality State	Indian Paintbrush	Meadowlark	1890

* Indicates one of the 13 original states

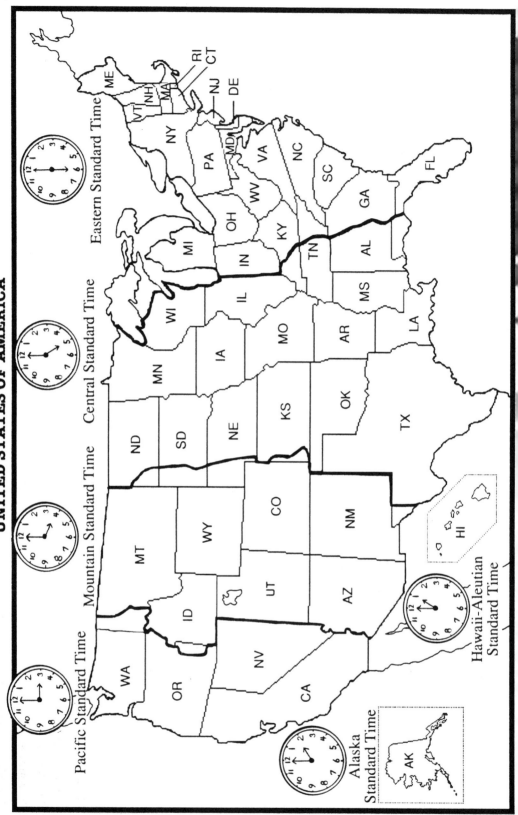

UNITED STATES OF AMERICA

Eastern Standard Time

Central Standard Time

Mountain Standard Time

Pacific Standard Time

Hawaii-Aleutian Standard Time

Alaska Standard Time

ME
VT
NH
MA
RI
CT
NY
NJ
DE
PA
MD
VA
WV
NC
OH
SC
KY
GA
MI
IN
TN
AL
WI
IL
MS
MN
IA
MO
AR
LA
ND
SD
NE
KS
OK
TX
MT
WY
CO
NM
ID
UT
AZ
NV
CA
OR
WA
HI
FL
AK

V

verb

A word that shows action or state-of-being (what the subject is).

Action	State-of-Being
sell	is
help	are
jump	am
eat	seem

✳ RULES

PRESENT TENSE

● In the present tense, verbs tell about something that happens or exists now.

● If the subject is first or second person singular, do not add an ending to the verb.

Examples:

I *swim* in the pool today.

You *run* in the park in the morning.

● If the subject is third person singular, add *s* to the verb.

Examples:

She *sings* today.

He *plays* baseball today.

Exception: Add *es* to verbs ending in *s*, *x*, *z*, *ch*, *sh*, or *ss*.

Examples: Cory *boxes* daily.

She *pushes* the stroller.

● If the subject is plural, do not add an *s* to the verb.

Examples:

We *swim* in the lake.

Sally and Kevin *exercise* daily.

Helping Verbs

● Some verbs have helping verbs.

Some Common Helping Verbs

am	do	might
are	does	must
can	is	shall
could	may	should

Example: Jack *should* eat his dinner.

● Some verbs in the present tense help the -*ing* form of the main verb and show continuing action.

Example: Eddie *is painting* the walls.

PAST TENSE

● In the past tense, verbs show something that has already happened. The letters *d* or *ed* are added to regular verbs to form the past tense.

Examples: bake   bak*ed*

jump   jump*ed*

● If a verb ends with a consonant followed by *y,* change the *y* to *i* and add *ed.*

Examples: worry   worr*ied*

hurry   hurr*ied*

fry   fr*ied*

● If a verb ends in a vowel followed by a consonant, double the consonant and add *ed.*

Examples: stop   stop*ped*

beg   beg*ged*

prefer   prefer*red*

omit   omit*ted*

Exceptions: enter   enter*ed*

offer   offer*ed*

Helping Verbs

● Use the helping verbs *has, have,* or *had* with the past participle form of a verb to show that something *happened in the past.*

Examples:

Sara *has played* ball before.

Paul and Kathy *have seen* that movie.

Karen *had showered* earlier.

verb, irregular

A verb that changes its spelling in the past tense and past participle form and does not have the *-ed* form.

SOME COMMON IRREGULAR VERBS

Present	Past	Past Participle
begin	began	begun
blow	blew	blown
bring	brought	brought
choose	chose	chosen
do	did	done
draw	drew	drawn
drink	drank	drunk
eat	ate	eaten
go	went	gone
grow	grew	grown
lay	laid	laid (to set)
lie	lay	lain (to rest)
ring	rang	rung
swim	swam	swum
wake	woke	woken

vertical line   A line that runs straight up and down, perpendicular to the horizon.

Example:

←—vertical line

volume   The amount of space inside a solid figure usually measured by a cubic centimeter, cubic inch, cubic foot, or cubic yard.

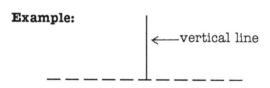

● To find the volume of a cube or rectangular prism, multiply the length times the width times the height.

$$V = L \times W \times H$$
$$V = 4" \times 2" \times 2"$$
$$V = 16 \text{ cu. in.}$$

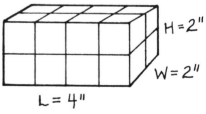

H = 2"
W = 2"
L = 4"

vowel   Any letter of the alphabet that is not a consonant and sometimes *w* and *y*.

Long Vowel Sounds		Short Vowel Sounds	
$\bar{a}$	$\bar{a}$pe	$\breve{a}$	c$\breve{a}$t
$\bar{e}$	$\bar{e}$qual	$\breve{e}$	h$\breve{e}$n
$\bar{i}$	$\bar{i}$ce	$\breve{i}$	p$\breve{i}$g
$\bar{o}$	$\bar{o}$pen	$\breve{o}$	$\breve{o}$tter
$\bar{u}$	$\bar{u}$se	$\breve{u}$	c$\breve{u}$b
$\bar{y}$	fl$\bar{y}$		

vowel digraph   Two vowels together that make one sound.

DIGRAPHS AND EXAMPLES

ai	**ee**	**oo**
tr*ai*n	gr*ee*n	b*oo*k
j*ai*l	f*ee*t	g*oo*d
au	**ew**	**ou**
c*au*ght	ch*ew*	*ou*t
h*au*nt	m*ew*	c*ou*ch
aw	**ie**	**ow**
p*aw*	p*ie*s	sn*ow*
cr*aw*l	cr*ie*s	b*ow*l
ay	**ie**	**ow**
pl*ay*	stor*ie*s	h*ow*
h*ay*	th*ie*f	c*ow*
ea	**oa**	**ue**
p*ea*ch	b*oa*t	gl*ue*
*ea*t	gr*oa*n	bl*ue*
ea	**oo**	**ui**
h*ea*d	m*oo*n	s*ui*t
br*ea*d	sp*oo*n	fr*ui*t

weather -
whether

The word *weather* refers to atmospheric conditions.

Example:

The *weather* will be cold and wet on Monday.

The word *whether* suggests a question.

Example:

I don't know *whether* she will go.

we're -
where - were

The word *we're* is a contraction that means *we are*.

Example:

We're in the kitchen.

The word *where* is an adverb that tells or asks location.

Example:

Do you know *where* the cat is?

The word *were* is a past tense form of the verb to be.

Example:

We *were* in school yesterday.

whole
number

An integer. Any number in the set (0, 1, 2, 3, ...)

Also see **integer**.

world

The earth. The world is round. The circumference of the world at the equator is 24,902 miles (40,075 kilometers). The circumference when measured around the world at the poles is 24,860 miles (40,007 kilometers).

Also see **map of world** on pages 140 and 141.

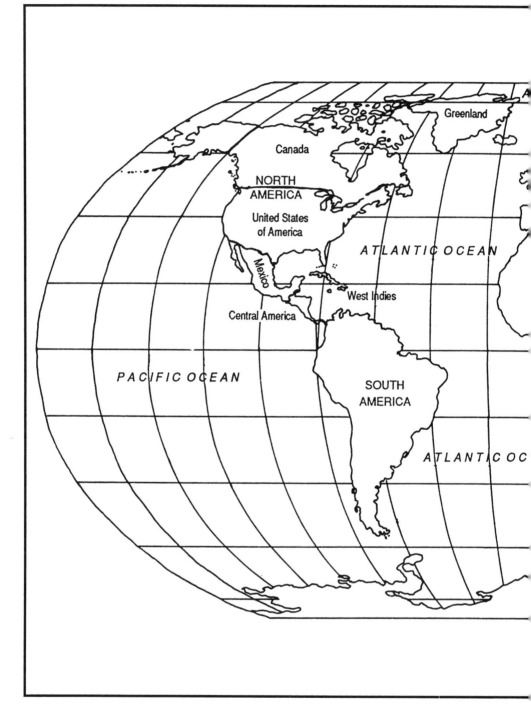

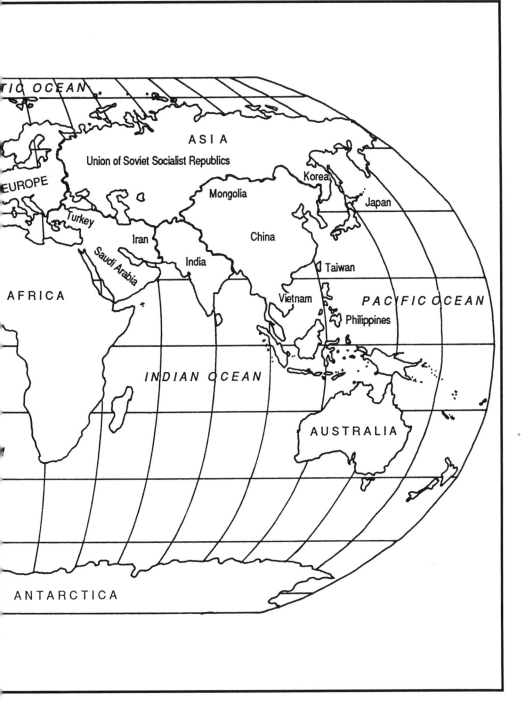

NOTES

NOTES

If you have any questions, comments, suggestions, or possible additions to offer **The KNOW IT ALL,** please let us know.

ZEPHYR PRESS

P.O. Box 13448

Tucson, AZ 85732-3448